In Loving Memory Of The Legend

Craig Ainsworth

(1985 - 2025)

Memoir Of A Celebrity Bodyguard

Contents

Introduction	3
Preface	5
Chapter 1: Introduction to Close Protection	7
Chapter 2: Training	16
Chapter 3: Military Protective Operations	27
Chapter 4: Out of the Ordinary	44
Chapter 5: Opulence	55
Chapter 6: Clients and Confidentiality	67
Chapter 7: Fun	81
Chapter 8: Awkward	91
Chapter 9: Relationships	111
Closing	120
Post Script	122

Introduction

What you hold in your hands is not fiction. It is a memoir, raw, unfiltered, and drawn directly from the front lines of a life lived behind secrecy. Being a bodyguard isn't just a career choice; it's a constant negotiation with danger, a profession shaped by split-second decisions, volatile environments, and powerful forces moving behind the curtain.

Every story in these pages is real. Nothing here is dressed up for drama or polished for effect. These are lived experiences, messy, unpredictable and unvarnished. I've written them not to impress, but to offer a rare glimpse into a world most people never see.

This is merely my story. There exist countless others, men and women, with narratives far more captivating than my own. But this one is mine to tell.

Enjoy

Preface

This book is unlike any you have ever encountered. Within its nine captivating chapters, I've shared over sixty-five stories that reveal the intriguing behind-the-scenes world of a celebrity bodyguard. Why are they top secret? Because of the private nature of the clientele that I've worked for, endless non-disclosure agreements, and due to the fact that speaking about our work is highly frowned upon. So, prepare to be shocked, awed, and horrified as you join me in these gripping experiences that have unfolded across the globe in a variety of extraordinary situations.

The field of close protection is frequently misinterpreted, with its truths hidden behind the glamour of Hollywood depictions or the silence of confidentiality agreements. This light-hearted and fun book (it is not just light and fun – it is also serious, awkward and sometimes even outrageous) aims to shed light on the reality of those intriguing individuals known as bodyguards, executive protection agents, or close protection officers, CPOs. For the benefit of the wider audience I will refer to our line of work as bodyguards and yes this will infuriate some seasoned agents reading this. Within this memoir lies a profession rich in complexity, accountability and empathy – an intricate balance between alertness and calm, obligation and secrecy. All client names have been excluded or altered, with identities concealed out of necessity. In a field as critical and unpredictable as security, anonymity serves as both a safeguard and a commitment, preserving the privacy of all involved whilst providing an unvarnished insight into this captivating domain.

The life of a bodyguard is filled with contradictions. It is a domain where the public's focus clashes with the reality of being an unsung hero. The magnifying glass is trained squarely on our every action. We shoulder a substantial burden of responsibility and therefore those in the inner circle are swift to judge, interrogate or belittle. Amongst our colleagues, the camaraderie is often tinged with a significant degree of criticism and conflict, creating an ongoing reality show of varying standards where everyone has their own approach, and deviating from it incurs derision.

Clients and principals may perceive us merely as human insurance policies or elevated couriers, babysitters, dog sitters, personal trainers, chefs, assistants or personal shopping assistants, yet the reality is vastly different. The most accomplished professionals exist in a perpetual state of hyper-vigilance, their minds operating at the pace of high-performance engines, anticipating threats that may evade others. Our world is one of discipline and unwavering focus, where the spotlight consistently evades us, remaining tantalizingly close.

This memoir explores the candid realities of a bodyguard's life, from navigating high-stakes assignments to the moral dilemmas that arise in moments of crisis. The journey is not merely about mastering tactical skills or embodying physical strength; it is about comprehending human behaviour, anticipating the unpredictable and making decisions where the stakes are nothing short of life-altering. Through candid storytelling, this book captures the adrenaline, the pressure and the ethical complexities that define our work.

Readers will step into a world where every moment counts, where safeguarding lives demands more than just a keen eye and swift reflexes. It demands resilience, integrity and an unwavering commitment to duty. As you turn these pages, may you come to appreciate the unseen guardian angels of close protection, those who operate behind the scenes yet bear the weight of their clients' safety on their shoulders. This is my account, a tribute to the dedication, sacrifice and quiet heroism of the bodyguard.

Chapter 1: Introduction to Close Protection

Origin

Before we dive into the juicy tales, I felt it important to share the origins of this profession (if you can't wait, please feel free to skip ahead to chapter 2), as it is not only a noble career choice but one of the oldest professions! The role of bodyguards has evolved over millennia, adapting to the shifting landscapes of power and protection. In ancient Egypt (c. 3000 BCE), pharaohs relied on elite warriors, such as the Medjay, to safeguard their reign. Similarly, in Mesopotamia (c. 2500 BCE), Sumerian and Akkadian kings surrounded themselves with loyal guards.

In ancient Greece (5th century BCE), Spartan kings were protected by the Hippeis, a prestigious unit of 300 warriors (just like the film which spawned a brutal workout), whilst Roman emperors, commencing with Augustus in 27 BCE, were shielded by the formidable Praetorian Guard. As medieval Europe emerged, knights and royal protectors (5th–15th century CE) stood watch over kings and nobles, whilst the Byzantine Varangian Guard, composed of Viking mercenaries, served as the personal security of emperors. In feudal Japan, from the 12th to 19th centuries, the samurai and shogunate bodyguards maintained the safety of powerful daimyōs and rulers.

With the dawn of the modern era, bodyguard services became increasingly structured, particularly in the 19th and 20th centuries, when political leaders, corporate moguls and high-profile figures sought specialised protection. The assassination of world leaders such as Abraham Lincoln in 1865 and John F. Kennedy in 1963 reinforced the need for professional security, giving rise to organisations like the U.S. Secret Service. Today, bodyguards are highly trained professionals, integrating intelligence, technology and strategy to ensure the safety of individuals in an unpredictable world. From the battle-hardened warriors of antiquity to the elite security specialists of today, the evolution of bodyguards reflects humanity's enduring need for protection in an ever-changing society.

Executive protection, as it is also known, has become an essential service in today's increasingly unpredictable world. The need for bodyguards arises from a variety of threats that individuals may face, particularly those in the public eye, such as celebrities, politicians and business leaders. These individuals often become targets of harassment, kidnapping, or even violence due to their high profile, wealth, or influence. The role of a bodyguard is to mitigate these risks and ensure the safety and security of their clients at all times.

The concept of bodyguards transcends mere physical presence; it involves a comprehensive approach to security that includes risk assessment, threat analysis and strategic planning. A bodyguard must evaluate potential threats in various environments, whether at public events, private engagements, or during travel. This analysis helps the bodyguard to develop and implement tailored security protocols that address the specific needs of their client while allowing them to maintain their lifestyle with minimal disruption. The effectiveness of bodyguards is rooted in their proactive nature, anticipating potential issues before they escalate into dangerous situations. The work of a bodyguard is intended to be uneventful without incident. If you come under fire, literally and figuratively speaking, then you've already failed because you didn't take the appropriate precautions to mitigate threats, naturally I'm referring to the incident in Pennsylvania 2024.

Another critical aspect of bodyguards is the relationship between the officer and the client. Trust and communication are paramount, as clients must feel confident in their protector's abilities and decisions. A successful bodyguard not only possesses the necessary skills and training to protect their client, but they also understand the nuances of human interaction. They must be skilled at interpreting body language, identifying signs of distress and preserving a tranquil, composed and collected bearing under duress. Cultivating this rapport is vital for establishing an ambience where clients can feel secure and concentrate on their duties rather than their protection.

Furthermore, the evolving nature of threats requires bodyguards to stay informed about current trends in security and technology. Advances in surveillance, communication and protective gear have transformed the field, enabling officers to respond more effectively to potential dangers. Continuous training and education in areas such as defensive driving, emergency medical response and situational awareness are vital for maintaining a high standard of protection. This commitment to professional development ensures that bodyguards are equipped to handle any situation that may arise.

In conclusion, the importance of bodyguards cannot be overstated. It serves as a vital safeguard for individuals who face unique risks due to their public status or personal circumstances. By combining thorough risk assessments with strong interpersonal skills and ongoing training, bodyguards play a crucial role in enhancing the safety and well-being of their clients. As the landscape of threats continues to evolve, the demand for skilled professionals in this field will likely increase, underscoring the ongoing relevance of bodyguards in an uncertain world. One thing is certain, I believe our occupations are safe from Terminator-style robots taking control any time soon.

Now in theory this all sounds very professional and some readers have a preconception of what may come but let me assure you what's about to be revealed over the coming pages is a far cry from what Hollywood's illusion has created!

A bodyguard's job isn't just about protection, it's a masterclass in juggling an entire ecosystem of personalities. From executive assistants and high-flying office executives to butlers, chauffeurs, spouses, children, pets and an endless stream of visitors, each individual holds the power to make your life either impossibly difficult or abruptly unemployed. The trick? Striking the perfect balance, engaging just enough to stay in their good books while guarding your principal's privacy like the Crown Jewels.

And then there's the job description, or lack thereof. Security? Of course. But in this profession, we're also errand boys, couriers to royalty, connoisseurs of outrageously expensive cheeses, personal shoppers, makeshift handymen assembling football nets, valets ensuring the Rolls-Royce gleams, and florists arranging exquisite bouquets. One minute, you're scanning for threats; the next, you're sourcing the world's most elusive luxury ice cream. The demands are endless, the tasks unpredictable, but such is the life of those who operate behind the scenes like protective ghosts.

The Why & The How

My journey into the world of close protection began at the age of fifteen, fuelled by a single moment of cinematic inspiration. Kevin Costner's portrayal of Special Agent Frank Farmer in *The Bodyguard*, alongside the late legendary Whitney Houston, planted a seed of ambition that would shape the course of my life. From that moment on, I knew what I wanted to become. But wanting something and being equipped for it are two very different things. At the time, I was a lanky, awkward teenager – tall, painfully skinny and riddled with acne. I bore an unfortunate resemblance to *Shaggy* from *Scooby-Doo*, and worse yet, I was an easy target.

Bullying was relentless. I was not just picked on, I was tormented. Even the school prefects, the so-called enforcers of discipline, partook in the torment. The worst of it? Two tomboys, brutal in their attacks. I was raised never to raise my fists against women, so I endured the beatings without resistance, suffering humiliation and anguish. On one occasion, as I struggled to escape, I pushed one of them off me and, by sheer accident, grazed her bosom in the process – a moment that only added to my misery as I fled the scene, ashamed and humiliated.

I hoped matters would change when I reached university. I enrolled in Exercise and Nutrition, determined to transform myself by building the strength and confidence I so desperately lacked, but instead of newfound respect, the bullying followed me. My efforts to bulk up only made me a bigger target. Until one day, everything changed.

One of my tormentors, a so-called semi-professional boxer decided to make me his next victim, but this time, I refused to be that helpless, skinny kid anymore. I fought back, and to my own surprise, I was the least bloodied and bruised out of the two of us. The feeling was indescribable, not just the physical victory, but the realization that I was not helpless and weak anymore. I could stand up for myself. And that moment, more than any film or dream, solidified my path forward. If I was going to be a protector, I had to first become someone worth respecting and looking the part.

Determined to turn that dream into reality, I embarked on a path that led me abroad, where I joined the Army. My commitment and drive eventually earned me a transfer to the Military Police, where I underwent the most rigorous and professionally structured training of my career. It was there that the foundation for my life in close protection was forged, one demanding discipline, resilience and an unrelenting pursuit of excellence.

The Role of a Bodyguard

The role of a bodyguard extends far beyond mere physical protection; it encompasses a wide range of responsibilities that require a unique skill set and a deep understanding of human behaviour. A bodyguard is often the first line of defence against potential threats, whether physical attacks, stalking or harassment. This role demands a high level of situational awareness, anticipating dangers before they manifest. Bodyguards must be adept at reading environments and people in order to identify warning signs that others might overlook. This acute awareness helps in formulating effective strategies to mitigate risks, ensuring the safety of the principal at all times.

Training is a fundamental aspect of a bodyguard's career. Many undergo rigorous physical training, including in areas such as self-defence techniques, weapons handling and emergency medical procedures. However, mental conditioning is equally important. Bodyguards learn to remain calm under pressure, making quick decisions in high-stress situations. This mental fortitude is essential when confronting potential threats or managing crises. Furthermore, continuous education on security protocols, legal issues and advances in technology are crucial, as the nature of threats evolves over time. A well-rounded bodyguard is equipped not only with physical skills but also with the knowledge necessary to adapt to changing circumstances. What sets the professionals apart from the rookies are the ones who have mastered NLP (Neuro Linguistic Programming) which is so vital in this career, including body language and second-guessing your client's every move to stay ahead of the curve.

Effective communication is another key component of a bodyguard's role. Since bodyguards often serve as the liaison between their principals and the outside world, they have to be able to convey information succinctly and clearly. This responsibility requires a high degree of professionalism and discretion, as bodyguards must navigate complex social dynamics while maintaining the confidentiality of their principals. Establishing trust is fundamental; a strong relationship allows the bodyguard to understand their principal's preferences and concerns, enabling a more tailored approach to their protection. This bond can significantly enhance the effectiveness of the security measures in place.

In addition to personal protection, bodyguards are often involved in logistical planning for events, travel and daily activities. This includes assessing venues for security vulnerabilities, co-ordinating with local law enforcement and developing emergency response plans. Their role is crucial in ensuring that all aspects of an outing are safe and secure. Bodyguards must also remain informed about the potential risks associated with different locations, including political climates, crime rates and cultural sensitivities. This comprehensive planning allows them to pre-emptively address any issues that may arise, creating a secure environment for their principal.

The life of a bodyguard is not without its challenges. The nature of the role can lead to long hours, irregular schedules and significant travel, which can strain personal life, health and certainly relationships. Moreover, the constant vigilance required can take a toll on a bodyguard's mental and emotional well-being. Despite these challenges, many find the role deeply rewarding. The ability to protect someone from harm, the thrill of navigating high-stakes environments and the camaraderie developed with clients often outweigh the difficulties. Ultimately, the role of a bodyguard is a complex blend of protector, confidant and strategist, making it a unique profession that requires dedication and resilience.

The Art of the Advance

The public and many clients often perceive the role of a bodyguard as effortless, observing only the polished exterior as we shadow our principals, whether trailing behind, walking alongside, or leading the way. However, the seamless execution of our duties belies the meticulous preparation required to ensure a client's safety and comfort, whether at a business meeting, a red-carpet event, or a hotel stay. The following outlines the rigorous process of conducting an advance, a cornerstone of professional close protection that demands precision, foresight, and adaptability.

The preparation begins well before the client's arrival. The first step is to identify the destination and establish contact with a designated point of contact at the venue. An initial meeting is arranged to facilitate introductions and gather critical information.

If the client is arriving by air, the advance team coordinates with the private terminal, ensuring the client's preferred vehicle is ready. The route from the terminal to the destination is driven and thoroughly assessed. Along the way, potential stops, such as parks or cafés the client may wish to visit are noted, as anticipating a client's preferences is integral to the role. The vehicle is meticulously prepared, stocked with items tailored to the client's comfort, including glass-bottled water, newspapers, magazines, chewing gum, charger cables, sweets, tissues, and hand sanitiser.

Next, the team identifies and maps the locations of the nearest hospital, police station, and fire station. For international assignments, the location of the client's national embassy is also confirmed. Each of these sites is visited to ensure familiarity with routes, enabling swift navigation in an emergency. At the venue itself, the advance team meets the point of contact to survey critical areas: the green room, safe room (if available), restrooms, and at least three viable exits. Familiarity with venue staff is established, and the optimal drop-off point is determined, ideally a discreet location, such as a basement entrance, to shield the client from public attention, paparazzi, or potential threats. This intimate knowledge of the venue enables rapid, informed decision-making should a crisis arise, as the adage "failing to prepare is preparing to fail" is a guiding principle in close protection.

For hotel stays, the client's room is configured to their exact specifications. This includes adjusting room temperature, blacking out intrusive lights for restful sleep, testing the room's ambience, and installing a panic alarm system. Again, the client's preferred brand of water and other amenities are provided to ensure comfort and familiarity.

Collaboration with venue security staff, where available, enhances efficiency by granting access to private entrances or elevators. Experienced protection officers memorise key details, venue facilities, operating hours, and even menu options to provide prompt, confident responses to client inquiries, thereby reinforcing professionalism and competence.

All gathered information is compiled into a comprehensive digital advance report, shared with the team. This report includes the client's itinerary, weather forecasts, traffic conditions, potential threats, major events in the area, and role-specific expectations. Each assignment is treated with the gravity of a mission, ensuring no detail is overlooked.

While every location presents unique challenges, and time constraints may occasionally limit the scope of an advance, this preparatory work remains a cornerstone of close protection. It is a process I have always found immensely rewarding, as it embodies the proactive diligence that defines our profession.

Chapter 2: Training

Anyone who's made it through this particular Military training course (I chose to omit the name in case I'd receive backlash) will tell you it's the stuff of legend – a brutal two-month ordeal that's undoubtedly the most intense close protection course in the world. I shall never forget the morning ritual of evacuating my bowels not once, but twice, before physical training even commenced. It was like my body was preparing for a war zone . . . by shedding every possible ounce of weight before the real pain kicked in. But hey, some recruits found their own shortcut by vomiting halfway through the workouts. Less weight, right?

Then, there was the secretive unit that'd show up during training exercises. We were so good at what we did that this special unit would even sneak a peek to see what and how we were operating. This wasn't just some two-month crash course, that was just the beginning. Before every deployment, our professional team would be selected and whipped into shape with another month of gruelling preparation. We were a finely tuned machine, ready for anything.

It's also super useful to have a mentor or someone you look up to or in this case down to due to his short stature, I'm referring to my then mentor and now friend "Frodo". Dynamite comes in small packages, he even received the coveted QCB (Queen's Commendation for Bravery) on operations.

And believe me when I say, we covered *everything*. Take, for instance, that memorable occasion we undertook live grenade training in the sweltering summer heat. Everything was bone dry, from the grass to the shrubs. So naturally, someone had the *brilliant* idea to lob both a smoke *and* a phosphorous grenade into the nearby bushes.

What happened next? Oh, nothing major – just the *entire* training range bursting into flames. We did our utmost to contain it, mind you. Chaps were chucking sand, jackets – even relieving themselves on the blaze in a valiant (if slightly undignified) attempt to halt the spread of the flames.

Next thing we know – fire brigade, local news, helicopters overhead filming what could have passed for a war zone. Safe to say, we made an impression. A rather smoky, flaming one. As the military adage goes, we 'popped smoke' and sheepishly returned to base ASAP.

Lights, Camera, Action!

I vividly recall one of the final details of our testing phase, an exercise that, unbeknownst to us, would turn into an all-out action scene. We were en route to an undisclosed location near a bustling ferry port, when we drove straight into an ambush worthy of a Hollywood blockbuster.

I was behind the wheel of the backup vehicle, following the VIP car closely, when suddenly, BOOM! An ear-splitting bang shattered the air, followed by a thick cloud of smoke. Without hesitation, my training kicked in. I instinctively manoeuvred around the VIP car, positioning myself to block a suspicious lorry that had pulled out in front of us. As I executed this move, the lorry's rear railing door burst open and out poured a crew of mock terrorists in ski masks, armed to the teeth. Our vehicle was declared immobile. Without missing a beat, I grabbed two smoke grenades to create a smokescreen for the VIP vehicle, allowing them to escape unhindered. In my haste, I failed to grab my ammunition bag, rookie mistake, leaving me with just a single full magazine for my Diemaco C8 rifle and my trusty sidearm, SIG Sauer P226 9mm.

I must say, the team worked like a well-oiled machine, extracting the VIP in record time. It's fascinating how tunnel vision kicks in when adrenaline floods your system everything sharpens, and you move on instinct. As we executed our escape, various masked 'terrorists' sprang up, shotguns in hand, forcing us to engage as we moved towards a secure area. One particular moment still makes me chuckle (and wince). In the heat of the moment, I found cover behind what I now know was a sleek, red civilian sports car. However, I hugged cover a little too tightly, resting the magazine butt of my rifle on the roof. Bad move as it left a nasty scratch as I returned fire. Costly lesson learnt: The training officer had to shell out to cover the damage!

To top it off, the entire dramatic spectacle played out in full view of ferry passengers behind the glass terminal. It was a training exercise to remember, brimming with adrenaline, errors and invaluable lessons. Who could have known a simple test run would feel like stepping into the midst of an action sequence?

Side note: Training serves a purpose, it enables us to learn from our mistakes. It is not a luxury, but a necessity. Embrace this mind-set and apply it to every aspect of your life to become your best version.

Instructor

Undoubtedly, one of the finest positions I've ever held was as an instructor in the unit, help training new recruits to become bodyguards for high-ranking generals deployed in some of the most hostile regions on the planet. The training was intense – range days, walking drills, tactical manoeuvres and high-speed driving exercises. But the most exhilarating part? Hands down, was when I had to don the infamous big red protective suit and engage in full-contact combat with the recruits, simulating real-world VIP defence scenarios.

Now, let's be clear – I took very little personal pleasure in pummeling fresh-faced recruits . . . But, hey, someone had to do it! It was a critical teaching moment, and if that meant taking a few well-placed swings, so be it. I still remember the sheer shock on one recruit's face before I knocked him completely unconscious – but don't worry, he was fine after a bit of recovery time. And then there was the time I nearly launched a recruit straight through a doorway and onto a settee mid-fight! It may sound severe and absolutely vital for a bodyguard to be able to defend himself and his client when the situation arises.

The most rewarding aspect of being an instructor, though, was undoubtedly orchestrating the final pass-out exercise, the ultimate test of everything the recruits had learnt. I had the privilege of working with an ultra-professional Scotsman, and together, we spent two months designing an exercise that was as close to real combat as possible. When it finally played out, it ran like absolute clockwork, earning us high praise from the training officer, a rare feat!

One of the most unforgettable scenarios we executed took place in one of London's most famous parks. The amount of planning, bureaucracy and red tape we had to cut through was staggering, but the payoff? Absolutely glorious. A full-blown, live-action blank round firefight erupted in the middle of the park, with stunned members of the public looking on. I had to reassure a few onlookers that they weren't witnessing a terrorist attack – just elite military training in action. Another standout exercise was staged inside a shopping mall after hours. The recruits were completely oblivious to the ambush we had set up, and when the simulated attack commenced, they were caught totally off guard. It was spectacular – chaos, gunfire (blanks, of course), and an intense battle unfolding between the 'terrorists' and our newly trained bodyguards.

Experiences like these stay with you for life. The adrenaline, the preparation, the split-second decision-making – it's all burnt into my memory.

Side note: Find passion in what you do, or risk resenting your vocation.

The Final Test

During the testing phase of our close protection (bodyguard) course, we travelled to an undisclosed location with our mock VIP in a two-vehicle convoy. The exercise was meticulously planned, and upon arriving at the gates of an exclusive country manor, we found that uniformed police officers with fake weapons had been hired to create a surreal atmosphere for this staged meeting. Everything unfolded as intended.

The 'VIP' was dropped off and greeted by the caretaker of the opulent mansion while my team and I positioned ourselves to provide 360-degree security coverage. As we stood outside, scanning the area for potential threats, I suddenly realised that I needed to relieve my near to bursting bladder. Not wanting to leave my post or trouble the staff, I hurriedly made my way to a nearby tree surrounded by bushes for some cover.

While keeping watch, I found myself unable to control the strong urge, and I ended up relieving myself in the garden, all the while anxious about possibly missing an attack. The tension of the moment made it difficult to compose myself. Eventually, I managed to regain my composure and returned to my position without having missed any action. As we were leaving the beautiful manor, the Directing Staff revealed that we had just visited the Prime Minister's Summer Vacation home. **WHAT!**

My face went pale, and I felt like a cartoon ghost. Those were real police officers, and the grounds were likely filled with security cameras. It hit me that there could be video footage in the Security Operations room of a nervous recruit bodyguard in a suit, excessively shaking his manhood, looking more like he was up to something else than simply relieving himself! In essence I Pi**ed in the Prime Minister's garden.

Side note: Make the most of challenging situations, after all, we're only human.

Civilian Training

It had always been a childhood dream of mine to complete a close protection course in the USA. After all, the silver screen made it look like the pinnacle of noble and heroic professions, saving lives, outsmarting villains and walking away from explosions without so much as a flinch. When I finally got the call from a well-established and reputable security agency in the good ol' US of A, I was equal parts hyped and petrified. Passing this course wasn't just a career milestone; it was personal. For ex-military types like me, transitioning into close protection should be a walk in the park. After all, we've already got the skills, just needed the final polish.

The course was a swift nine days (entry level), and to my immense delight (and questionable luck), I was paired with a hoofing Royal Marine who had established himself as a legend in his own right. Let me tell you, I laughed so hard during that course that I practically developed a six-pack. By the end, my abs were thanking him more than my instructor.

The course itself was no picnic, though. We covered everything: Close-quarter combat, death-by-PowerPoint presentations, scenario drills, simunition scenarios (similar to paintball but the rounds have plastic projectiles with paint which stings like a wasp) and bonding moments with attack dogs who clearly took their job descriptions very seriously.

But one particular element stood out as the pièce de résistance of misery: the Pepper Spray scenario.

Now, I'd been through CS gas training with the military, so I thought, *How bad can this be?* Spoiler alert: I was an idiot. Mildly cocky and joking right up until the moment, I decided to open my mouth and eyes mid-spray – because why not make it a spectacle? The instructor, already irritated by my antics, did not hold back. One generous rip of the spray later, my life descended into utter chaos.

For thirty agonising minutes, I couldn't breathe. My face was on fire, my soul tried to leave my body, and I was convinced this was my dramatic Hollywood exit. I begged them to call an ambulance, flailed like a wounded seal and cursed every decision that led me to that moment. Their solution? A 'fine mist spray' of water to 'help alleviate the burning sensation'. A fine joke is what it was. My eyes didn't just water – they saw my life flash before them. Upside down, inside out, through a kaleidoscope of pain.

But wait, it gets better. Just as I thought the worst was behind me, they announced pool drills. A nice swim test to cool off, right? Wrong. The moment we hit the water, the pepper spray reignited. Imagine diving into a pool only to find yourself back in the fiery depths of hell. Unbelievable. Naturally it wasn't as bad as the initial experience although we were reminded that you will respect pepper spray!

Side note: Take it from me, police-grade pepper spray is no joke, especially if a pool is involved afterwards.

Aspirations

After completing rigorous training, the only goal left is to secure a position with a reputable security firm, a gateway to both a rewarding career and a steady income. Yet, the real thrill lies in the mystery: Who will you protect, and will fortune smile upon you with bonuses and tips?

In your early days, as a fledgling agent, you'll start in the operations room. There, you'll immerse yourself in the intricacies of your client's daily existence, absorbing every detail like a student of life. As you prove your mettle, you'll transition to roles that require more mobility, first behind the wheel, then into more advanced tasks. With experience, you'll evolve into the primary protective force, handling the most critical assignments. Mastery of these roles will eventually lead to travel duties, and when you're truly proficient, you'll command your own protection detail.

For those who climb the ranks within a security firm, the pinnacle of achievement is leading a brand-new team, designing, managing and executing operations from the ground up. However, excelling in this industry demands more than just technical expertise; it requires a resilience of spirit and a tough, unyielding skin. Criticism can come from every direction, from high-profile clients and influential executive assistants (whom you must treat with the deference of a client, given their considerable power) to house managers, butlers, contractors, guests and even your peers. Every move is intensely scrutinised, making this one of the most high-pressure careers imaginable.

Even when you execute a thousand tasks flawlessly, a single misstep or a poor judgement call can place you on the chopping block, potentially ending your career in an instant. This is not a vocation for the faint-hearted. It demands an ironclad mindset, impeccable physical fitness, relentless self-motivation, and an unyielding drive to succeed. Mastering the art of stress management is crucial; the faster you hone this skill, the more effortlessly you'll navigate the challenges of the role. With practise, problem-solving becomes second nature, and anticipating future challenges becomes the key to thriving in this unforgiving field.

Side note: While some may choose a profession driven by misguided intentions, your strength lies in staying grounded in your values and true to who you are.

Fitness

As far as fitness goes, I really believe that CrossFit has the best applications for close protection training. It's the perfect way to prepare recruits, keep current protectors in shape, and challenge oneself regularly. My South African colleague Gregory was incredible at it, and he introduced some awesome WODs (workout of the day) as part of our training for new recruits. Trying to keep up with him was a challenge, he was in a league of his own, built for it with the right mindset, fitness and skills. I'll always remember the time when I completed a WOD called Murph. It was quite the experience!

The Murph CrossFit workout was named after Lieutenant Michael P. Murphy, a U.S. Navy SEAL who was posthumously awarded the Medal of Honour for his heroic actions during Operation Red Wings in Afghanistan in 2005.

Lt. Murphy, known as 'Murph' to his teammates, sacrificed his life to save his fellow SEALs while under heavy enemy fire. Despite being severely wounded, he exposed himself to enemy fire to make a call for help, ultimately leading to the rescue of Marcus Luttrell, the sole survivor of the mission.

Murphy was known for doing this workout, which he originally called 'Body Armor', as part of his training. It consisted of a 1-mile run, 100 pull-ups, 200 push-ups, 300 air squats and another 1-mile run for good measure in a 20-pound weighted vest.

Gregory really took it up a notch by turning the 1-mile run into an uphill challenge before and after the bodyweight exercises! I honestly can't believe I finished this WOD; it was the closest I've ever come to throwing up and, without a doubt, the hardest I've ever trained!

Another exercise set I've literally performed over a hundred times was called the 300 as mentioned before in the intro.

The '300 Workout' is a legendary fitness routine made famous by the actors and stuntmen who trained for the 2006 film *300*, where they portrayed Spartan warriors. The workout was designed by Mark Twight, a former elite climber and trainer, to build incredible strength, endurance and a shredded warrior-like physique.

The workout consists of 300 total reps, performed as quickly as possible with no scheduled rest between exercises.

- 25 Pull-ups
- 50 Deadlifts (135 lbs / 60 kg)
- 50 Push-ups
- 50 Box Jumps (24-inch box)
- 50 Floor Wipers (135 lbs barbell / 60 kg, alternating legs)
- 50 Kettlebell Clean and Press (25 reps per arm, 36 lbs / 16 kg KB)
- 25 Pull-ups

During my second tour in Afghanistan, I did this workout so many times that I ended up injuring both my biceps for over a year. Luckily, a girlfriend at the time who happened to be an osteopath helped me recover in just three sessions! A huge shout-out to osteopaths! Staying fit, mobile and prepared is essential. It really makes everything easier, especially when we can be on our feet for days. Plus, it keeps us healthy!

Side note: Exercise isn't optional, it's fundamental to who we are. Vital for our mindset and health, it taps into the innate resilience and adaptability of the human body. We are meant to push ourselves.

Chapter 3: Military Protective Operations

Conducting close protection operations in war zones is the ultimate test of endurance, skill and character. It's not just a job, it's a relentless mission that demands every ounce of one's being. These six-month tours aren't for the faint of heart. Every single day is spent executing flawless operations, with only a brief two-week window for rest and recovery halfway through, which, to be honest, feels more like a mirage in the desert.

But the real challenge? Living shoulder to shoulder with the same team day in and day out, in an environment where tension is the only constant. The pressure is intense, the stakes are high and the daily grind tests you in ways that most can't comprehend. It forces you to become not just a professional but a master of human dynamics, a true people person, capable of reading the room and adapting to any situation.

There are moments in those tours that I will forever cherish, moments that no words could ever fully capture. The camaraderie, the shared purpose, the feeling that you and your team are the last line of defence for someone's life, it's a bond unlike any other. It's hard to explain to those who haven't lived it, but those experiences are etched into your soul, transforming you into something more than just a bodyguard; they shape you into a well-rounded individual, prepared for anything life throws your way. The lessons, the training, the sweat and sacrifices, they stay with you for ever, becoming a part of who you are.

First Day

It was my first day on close protection duty in the Middle East, and the air was thick with dust and tension as we prepared to welcome the incoming General whose life we were ultimately responsible for. This wasn't just any assignment; this was a six-month mission to safeguard a high-ranking military leader in a region rife with unpredictability. Months of preparation had culminated in this moment, every detail meticulously planned from a military perspective. Routes were scouted, contingencies drafted, and every step rehearsed with precision. Nothing, or so we thought, had been left to chance.

The day began with a buzz of controlled mayhem. We were assigned two drivers from the Logistics Corps as our primary navigational assets. Driving in Afghanistan was simply chaotic - there's no place like it. The route had been carefully plotted, the convoy briefed, and now it was time to meet the General himself. To our surprise, he was affable and warm, a demeanour that momentarily eased the nervous energy humming within the team.

As we set off, every mile felt like a test of our capabilities. The convoy moved with the kind of fluid precision that only comes from rigorous training. But as we approached the meeting location, threading our way through the heavily secured perimeter, disaster struck. The gates were narrower than anticipated, and in a moment of hesitation, the car scraped hard against the edge. The sound was sickening, a metallic screech that seemed to echo in slow motion.

We froze. In an instant, the atmosphere shifted from controlled professionalism to sheer mortification. The convoy halted as the General stepped out, his expression unreadable, while the sharp eyes of surrounding close protection teams from other nations zeroed in on us. The source of the commotion became painfully clear, a deep scrape ran along the left side of the vehicle, and the rear left taillight dangled precariously by a few strained wires.

The driver, eyes wide with shock, sat paralysed, remaining in his seat with his hands gripping the ten and two position. I could almost see the stream of panicked thoughts racing through his mind. With no time to waste, we scrambled into damage-control mode. A roll of duct tape materialised like a lifeline, and we patched up the vehicle as best as we could. The General, to his credit, said nothing, but the weight of the moment pressed heavily on us.

In hindsight, that scrape was more than just a mark on the vehicle; it was a humbling lesson in the unpredictable nature of human error. No amount of planning or preparation can account for every variable. And for the driver? That day wasn't just a rough start, it was a baptism by fire into the unforgiving world of close protection.

Side note: Always carry tape with you—it's a versatile tool with countless uses. I rely on it often!

Some 'Light' Hiking

The glamorous life of a military close protection detail in Kabul, where every day feels like an action set, except with more sweat and fewer Oscars. Allow me to recount the absurd tale of our mountain 'adventure' with the General. What was meant to be a routine visit quickly turned out to be what felt like a scene out of Sylvester Stallone's film *Cliffhanger*.

We approached the airspace in a couple of Blackhawk helicopters close to the Pakistan border; the mountains were quite the spectacle, reaching high into the blue heavens. The mission was simple on paper: accompany the General on a 'strategic' fortified and essential meeting in a very secluded spot in the east of Afghanistan. The stakes? High. The altitude? Higher. The plan? Let's just say it involved climbing something that felt taller than Mount Olympus, courtesy of an overly enthusiastic American soldier's exaggerated pep talk. Spoiler: The 'tour guide' was not very forthcoming.

Enter my colleague, whom we'll call Denzel, because his resemblance to a young Denzel Washington was uncanny. Tall, strong, and so effortlessly cool, you'd expect him to be the hero of this tale. But no one looks cool lugging an underslung grenade launcher up a mountain in full battle gear. Let's not forget my own load, which included enough equipment to make me a walking military surplus store. Denzel and I were equipped for war, not a scenic hike.

Meanwhile, the General, and his entourage looked like they were on a casual day out, shedding layers and carrying 'light loads' as if they were headed for a picnic. Denzel and I exchanged a look that said, this is going to suck, and began our ascent, determined to hide just how much our gear and pride were killing us.

The climb quickly devolved into a symphony of pain. My quadricpes burned, my lungs screamed and my dignity was hanging on by a thread. Sweat poured down my face in rivulets as we trudged along, each step a Herculean effort under 25 kilograms of gear. Denzel was silent but visibly suffering. We weren't just hiking; we were dragging ourselves up that mountain like reluctant sherpas. The hardest part was trying to hide our anguish from the General; couldn't show an ounce of weakness.

And then, just when we thought we couldn't look any more pathetic, a group of local kids darted past us, barefoot and laughing. Barefoot. These pint-sized kids bounded up the treacherous terrain like mountain goats as if it were a flat football pitch. If their altitude mastery wasn't humbling enough, the laughter in their eyes as they glanced back at us, two sweaty, gear-laden giants, sealed the deal. They were moving so fast that I'm pretty sure they lapped us.

At the summit, we finally caught our breath, pretending we hadn't just experienced what felt like a near-death cardio session. The General, meanwhile, looked completely unfazed, casually surveying the horizon. We took turns to step out of view in order to catch our breath back as we were gasping for the little oxygen that was available to us at altitude.

So, what did we learn? That physical fitness is crucial, pre-mission training is underrated, and sometimes, humour is your best weapon against absurdity. Because if you're going to climb a mountain in full battle gear, you'd better have quads of steel and a sense of humour strong enough to survive the journey, or at least the sight of laughing kids racing past you like you're standing still.

Side note: In many situations, it's not physical strength but mental resilience that makes the difference, no matter your fitness level.

Near Miss

On this particular solo detail with the General, I was tasked with accompanying him to a critical meeting with local leaders and elders in Wardak Province. Little did I know how narrowly we would escape what could have been a devastating outcome.

The mission was set to begin with a flight aboard a Chinook helicopter, the massive twin-rotor aircraft known for its thunderous presence. Only one close protection operative could accompany the General on this trip, and as fate would have it, I almost missed the flight thanks to a last-minute battle with pre-mission nerves. Thankfully, I made it just in time, my mind racing with the weight of the responsibility ahead.

Upon arrival, we were escorted through a network of pathways to a compound where the high-stakes discussions were to take place. The atmosphere initially seemed secure, with a formidable show of force. Generals from my country, the USA and Australia were present, flanked by a sea of soldiers providing 360-degree protection. Helicopters hovered above, ensuring air cover and every approach to the compound was guarded. The presence of such overwhelming security gave us a sense of reassurance, a rare luxury in such volatile conditions. Boy, was I mistaken!

The compound itself was a simple structure, open to the sky, with no roof to shield us from potential threats. While the Generals engaged with the elders in the heart of the compound, security teams occupied the entrances and scattered strategically around the perimeter. The sun beat down relentlessly, draining our energy as the meeting stretched on. Eventually, even the most disciplined among us relented, taking a moment to sit and recover from the oppressive heat.

It was then that absolute mayhem erupted. Without warning, a Rocket Propelled Grenade (RPG) streaked directly overhead, its unmistakable whoosh slicing through the air just above the meeting party. The tranquil scene shattered instantly as every Protective Security Detail (PSD) operative sprang into action. Soldiers shouted commands and an Australian Special Forces operative dragged his colleague to safety with a calm urgency that belied the chaos around us. Chairs clattered to the ground as we scrambled for cover, instinctively reacting to the threat.

One of my colleagues, assigned to protect his General, bolted towards the meeting area, his face etched with panic as he sought shelter under the pergola. Meanwhile, I found myself alone, patrolling the compound wall where the RPG had been launched. Adrenaline coursed through me as I scanned the horizon, my senses heightened to a razor's edge. It was an eerie moment standing guard by myself, aware of the harrowing fragility of our position.

The aftermath was a sobering reminder of how quickly a seemingly secure situation could descend into carnage. The attack could have gone wrong in so many ways, and yet, by some stroke of fortune, it did not. The close call left us all shaken but resolute, a stark lesson in the unpredictable and perilous nature of our work.

Side note: A false sense of security can be deceiving, stay vigilant and do not fall prey to its illusion.

Trigger Fingers

During the height of the Afghanistan war, I found myself riding shotgun on a high-stakes mission. Our team was tasked with protecting an esteemed four-star General, a man whose decisions carried enormous weight in the ongoing conflict. Beside me in the driver's seat was a legendary Royal Marine, serving as our protection driver for this critical assignment. Known for his steel nerves and razor-sharp instincts, he had earned a reputation for tackling challenges head-on.

On this particular day, we had just concluded a vital meeting at a U.S. military base. Time was against us, and we needed to return to our own base without delay for an even more consequential rendezvous. The urgency was palpable; every second weighed against the backdrop of war.

As we exited the U.S. camp, our mission hit an unexpected snag: a massive U.S. Army convoy stretched out before us, an ironclad procession that brought our plans to a grinding halt. Our base was tantalisingly close, just around the corner, but the convoy's sheer length and rigidity threatened to delay us indefinitely.

The Royal Marine, true to his fearless reputation, decided to gamble. With nerves of steel, he seized an opening and manoeuvred our armoured Toyota Land Cruiser into the convoy, cutting through the U.S. convoy's rigid formation. It was a decision that immediately backfired. In a war zone, surprises are unwelcome, and anything outside the norm, especially a non-American vehicle breaching a U.S. convoy is considered a threat.

What happened next unfolded in a heartbeat yet felt like an eternity. Suddenly, we found ourselves directly behind a fortified Humvee. Perched atop its turret were two soldiers, their eyes scanning the horizon for any hint of danger. Our intrusion triggered alarm bells. One of the American soldiers spotted us and immediately began shouting, his gestures unmistakably signalling us to halt. Our Marine, however, maintained course, determined to push through.

In an instant, the situation escalated. The turret gunner's warnings were replaced by decisive action. He drew his sidearm, a compact but menacing 9mm pistol, and aimed it squarely at us. My mind raced with the possibility of a tragic 'blue-on-blue' – the horrifying scenario where allied forces mistakenly engage one another.

Acting on instinct, I grabbed the General's four-star banner and held it high, a desperate attempt to signal our identity and importance. But instead of diffusing the tension, the gesture seemed to fuel the soldier's fury. His face contorted with anger, and I watched in disbelief as he cocked his pistol. Did he realise that his sidearm posed little threat to the armour-clad Land Cruiser we occupied? It didn't matter. A single mistake, a fraction of a second's hesitation, and this could have spiralled into disaster.

Recognising the volatility of the moment, we made a split-second decision to pull off to the side of the road. It was a tactical retreat, a measure to avoid provoking the situation further while allowing tempers to cool. The atmosphere was electric, the tension almost suffocating. This was the reality of war: split-second decisions, razor-thin margins and the constant hum of danger lurking in every shadow.

The convoy passed, the American soldier's weapon lowered, and we resumed our journey. But the memory of that moment lingered, a stark reminder of the unpredictable nature of war. It was an encounter that underscored the fragility of alliances under pressure and the ever-present need for calm amidst the storm. In the end, we made it to our base unscathed, but the lesson was clear: in the theatre of war, even the smallest miscalculation can ignite a firestorm.

Side note: Patience is a virtue.

The Beyond

When you stay in this profession long enough, you bear witness to things most people could never comprehend. There are moments of wonder, of bizarre unpredictability, but there is also horror, grief and loss. In conflict zones, death is not an abstraction. It is not something distant. It comes for colleagues, for friends and for the innocent. And no amount of experience can ever prepare you for the weight of it.

An unforgettable scenario unfolded in Kabul, Afghanistan, on an afternoon like any other. We were in the follow vehicle, trailing the VIP convoy, scanning the surroundings for any sign of danger. My role was to watch, to anticipate, to call out any threats, because in a place like that, every second counts. I was seated in the back, eyes trained on the road behind us, ensuring nothing and no one encroached on our movement unnoticed. We were nearly at the camp. The road behind us was clear, empty, quiet. And then, absolute hell. A boy, no older than seven or eight, ran into the street. He wasn't looking at us. He wasn't looking at anything but the ball he was chasing. A simple, innocent moment, one that should have meant nothing. But there, on that road, at that time, it meant everything. From the opposite direction came a Turkish Medical APC (Armoured Personnel Carrier), a towering armoured vehicle with a sharp, unforgiving bonnet. It was moving too fast, too heavy, and had no chance to stop.

Time didn't slow down. It didn't pause. There was no cinematic delay, no moment to react. One second, the boy was there. The next, he was gone. The impact was absolute. The sharp edged bonnet of the APC struck him directly in the head, ending his life in an instant. I called it in as it happened, my voice hollow and mechanical, as if saying the words could somehow make them less real. But nothing could change the reality of what I had just witnessed. The most tragic irony of all, it was a medical team. A team meant to heal, to save lives. And yet, in that moment, there was nothing they could do.

A crowd gathered almost immediately, their cries and anguish filling the air. The loss of a child is unbearable anywhere in the world but in a place already drowning in sorrow, it feels even heavier. The story made the local news the next day, reduced to a headline, a passing tragedy in a country too familiar with death.

For those of us who saw it, who lived it, it was more than that. It was a moment that lingered. A moment that never really faded. And the saddest truth of all? It wasn't rare. Accidents like this happen in war zones more often than anyone wants to admit. A child, a ball, a road and a country too broken to stop it.

Side note: Continual exposure to traumatic events inevitably dulls emotional sensitivity, gradually eroding

empathy and, over time, the very essence of one's humanity.

In Stitches

As our first military close protection tour in Kabul wrapped up, we were finally given a golden ticket, a proper farewell bash, courtesy of our colleagues at the Embassy inside the green zone. The venue? The Ambassador's living quarters. The invite came with one strict condition: no weapons. Apparently, a room full of highly trained, battle-hardened men and an open bar was already a risky enough combination. After six months of relentless grafting, with zero alcohol and nothing but sand, sweat and stress for company, we weren't about to turn down a well-earned drink.

The night arrived. We ditched our military uniforms for whatever civilian attire we could scrape together, at this point, anything that wasn't camouflage felt like a tuxedo. Our embassy hosts welcomed us with open arms, and before I could even find a seat, the beer and wine were flowing like the Kabul River in monsoon season. Strangely, I decided to stay sober, maybe it was instinct, maybe it was fate, maybe it was just dumb luck. My marine colleague, Clint, on the other hand, went full Viking. Every drop he drank seemed to hit him like a direct artillery strike, and within record time, he was *jolly*. Very, very jolly.

Then, to our absolute delight, we noticed something we hadn't seen in six months: women. Yes, actual, real-life women. And let me tell you, after half a year in a war zone, your brain plays tricks on you. That plain-looking admin assistant? Your mind transforms her into a Victoria's Secret model. That friendly logistics officer? Suddenly, she's an exotic Bond girl. The war-zone goggles were on full power.

At one point, I heard a blonde whisper to her friend, *'He doesn't know I like him'* while sneaking a glance in my direction. Cue internal panic. I was about to turn, about to engage, about to potentially end my dry tour with a little romantic victory when – *boom* – Clint happened. Our *jolly* Marine came flying in, singing, dancing and with the grace of a wrecking ball, he dragged me straight into his charade. He had been training so hard that he decided it was the perfect time to start picking up fully grown men over his head. For reasons unknown, others started returning the favour. The room turned into an impromptu Strongman contest.

And then, it happened. Clint, in his drunken, overly enthusiastic state, somehow lost balance and went down headfirst akin to a tranquillised giraffe. A loud *crack* echoed through the room. He stood up, blinking, confused with a massive gaping wound smack between his eyes. Blood started pouring down his face. Instantly, the party transformed into a medical emergency. We couldn't exactly waltz into an Afghan hospital unless we fancied an impromptu kidnapping, so the embassy's medic stepped in. Clint, being Clint, was completely oblivious to the fact that his face now resembled a badly stitched-up football. I had to physically restrain him just so the medic could get the needle through his forehead. The man was grinning the entire time, like he had just won the lottery, not lost a pint of blood.

With the party officially ruined by Clint's forehead explosion, it was time to get back to base. Our transport? Gone. Instead, the brilliant solution was to throw me and my freshly stitched-up Marine mate into an Afghan taxi and hope for the best. Now, let me paint you a picture: two blonde, pale, clearly Western blokes in an unarmoured local taxi outside the safety of the green zone in the middle of Kabul at night. If our driver was working for the Taliban or Al-Qaeda, this story would have ended in a ransom video. It was, without exaggeration, one of the dumbest security breaches I had ever been part of.

By some miracle, we made it back without being sold to the highest bidder. The next morning, as we prepared to leave for home, Clint looked like Frankenstein's monster with his stitched-up forehead. We laughed about it all the way to Dubai, where we *probably* should have taken him straight to a plastic surgeon. I still have the photographs of Clint the morning after; looking like he had lost a pub fight with a sledgehammer. And whilst I didn't get my war-zone love story that night, I did get one heck of a memory.

Side note: If you don't respect alcohol, it will disrespect you with vengeance.

Dark Tourism

During a protective tour in the Middle East, our team was assigned to a high-ranking General, a man who, in addition to his military prowess, fancied himself an adventurous hiker. Lucky us, we were stationed in a region surrounded by mountains. The catch? Those mountains weren't in a national park, they were smack in the middle of a war zone. Naturally, it was only a matter of time before the General declared, 'Let's go for a stroll up that mountain'. Because why wouldn't you want a little cardio in a combat zone?

This wasn't just any mountain, either. It came with a list of hazards that would make a health-and-safety officer faint. We conducted all the usual advance work: reconnaissance, precautionary checks, route planning, but let's be real, preparation only takes you so far when danger lurks around every corner. In hindsight, it's fair to ask: What were we thinking?! Although our General certainly had a lot of faith in us as his protection team to wander about Kabul for a stroll. The adventure began in the capital city, where VBIEDs

(Vehicle-Borne Improvised Explosive Devices) were unwelcome guests on every street. Driving there was no Sunday cruise; it was more like an extended panic attack on wheels. Our heads were on a constant swivel, scanning every vehicle, alleyway and suspicious-looking locals as we navigated our way to the mountain.

When we finally arrived, we were greeted not by serene nature but by a pack of feral, rabid-looking dogs that seemed to have a personal vendetta against us. Their snarls made it clear we were not welcome, so we scrambled past them and reached the foot of the mountain trail. That's when the real fun began.

Now, let me explain why I call this the 'death hike'. Half of the mountain was riddled with landmines because, apparently, Mother Nature and modern warfare decided to collaborate on an extreme adventure course. A thin wire fence decorated with charming skull-and-crossbones signs separated the so-called safe path from certain doom. And calling it a 'path' was generous, it was more like a tightrope of gravel daring you to misstep.

We carefully picked our way along this narrow trail, hearts pounding and eyes glued to the ground as though staring harder might somehow make the landmines disappear. By the time we reached the summit, we were equal parts exhilarated and terrified. The view over the desolate city was,. . well, breathtaking in its own apocalyptic way. But let's be honest, the real victory was that none of us had blown ourselves up.

The descent was just as harrowing, with every step back down feeling like a victory in itself. Once we made it to the base, past the rabid dogs, and back into our vehicles, we drove back to base with a mix of relief and disbelief.

Looking back now, I can't decide what's more shocking: that the General thought this was a great idea or that we agreed to go along with it. But hey, that's close protection for you, protecting your principal, one landmine-riddled hike at a time.

Side note: There's something strangely invigorating about walking the proverbial tightrope between life and death, though it's not an experience I would ever deliberately pursue.

A Night at the Serena

So there I was solo, geared up, and mentally rehearsing my "don't shoot the Dutch" protocol. Our General had received an invitation from his Dutch counterpart for a diplomatic dinner at the once-iconic Serena Hotel in Kabul, now under new, less-than-hospitable management (The Taliban).

This wasn't your typical meat-and-potatoes detail. Only one of us could fit into the Dutch protection detail, and naturally, the honour (or the short straw) fell to me. Thankfully, the Dutch were legends, equal parts trained killers and stand-up comedians. Deadly efficient, but also a lot of fun... the kind of folks who could run a security cordon and host a barbecue at the same time.

To prepare, I did my homework. I studied their SOPs like I was cramming for a final examination in "Dutch Tactical Awesomeness 101," memorised their protocols, and even familiarised myself with their weapons, because, let's be honest, if the party turned into a live-action Die Hard sequel, I'd need to know which end goes boom.

Given the nature of the venue, I was required to maintain a discreet profile with my equipment. No heavy ordnance. Merely my reliable Sig Sauer P226 concealed, and a mischievous 9mm Heckler & Koch submachine gun concealed within my messenger bag. You know, just enough to politely return fire should things get lively.

Now, the Serena Hotel, formerly a symbol of luxury, was in what we affectionately called the "red zone"." Translation: the kind of place where "anything could happen" wasn't just a warning, it was a lifestyle. That night, though, it looked like the UN's version of a prom night. Security details from every flavour of NATO were milling around, French, Americans, Italians, Germans, Brits. A veritable smorgasbord of accents, weapons, and suspicious glares.

And then… She walked in. Or, more accurately, *she was already there*. A striking blonde woman sitting solo in the lobby, looking like she had wandered out of a Milan fashion show and accidentally into a covert ops summit. Croatian, we later learnt. Also completely unphased by the sea of heavily armed, overly alert, mildly sweaty men around her.

Now, understand the scene: hardened professionals, all scanning, all assessing, everyone pretending not to notice *her* while definitely noticing her. The room was tense. Eyes were sharp. Triggers were half-cocked. Then... the finger food arrived.

And just like that, the Germans broke ranks like a linebacker squad hearing the dinner bell. Plates were flying, mini quiches disappearing faster than you could say "schnitzel." It was quite comical, a snack-fuelled frenzy.

I saw my moment. Casually, diplomatically, *professionally*, I strolled over to the Croatian mystery lady and introduced myself. (Calm down, I had a girlfriend at the time. This was purely MI6-style icebreaking.) The next thing you know, one by one, every other operator in the room started drifting over, like moths to a very glamorous, very unexpected flame. She became the accidental belle of the ballistic ball.

The rest of the night went off without a hitch. The General schmoozed, speeches were made, nobody got shot, and we even made it back to base with all limbs and dignity intact. Mission accomplished, and the General was pleased. As for me? I survived a solo detail, infiltrated a Dutch operation, and witnessed the international language of diplomacy: hors d'oeuvres and a pretty woman.

Side note: Spoils of war, so to speak.

Chapter 4: Out of the Ordinary

You can only *imagine* the kind of things a bodyguard gets to see, experience, and unfortunately, get exposed to. We're not just hired muscle; we're trusted with the *inner circle,* the VIPs, the power brokers, the ones who need to keep their lives safe from the madness they've created. And let me tell you, 'experiencing everything' is an understatement. We're expected to do near literally *anything* and *everything,* whether holding back a crowd, cleaning up the aftermath of a wild party or transporting over fifty pieces of luggage across the world like a high-end courier service. And if you can't hack it? Well, you're probably getting a one-way ticket to your next gig. No questions asked.

Now, as much as we get to rub shoulders with celebrities, jet-set across the world, and dine at restaurants that make the average person's jaw drop, there's also a *dull side* to this glamorous lifestyle. You see, for every private jet and five-star dinner, there's an equal amount of mind-numbing boredom, soul-crushing austerity, and on occasion, disgust. It's not all champagne and caviar; sometimes, it's just *waiting* in a cold, sterile room while your charge decides which five-star hotel to *actually* stay at. Forget the VIP treatment; at times, you're more like the world's most underpaid babysitter. And honestly, the next time someone mentions 'luxury', just remember, sometimes it's just a fancy word for *expectation.*

Baptism of Fire

In my first week on a brand-new detail, I was introduced to the team, a solid bunch, except for one sneaky Northerner. We'll keep his name under wraps. This particular night, I was assigned to an evening detail, escorting a stunningly beautiful heiress to a club in London. She was a household name, and her presence in the VIP section was nothing short of a spectacle. Pat, a no-nonsense, tough-as-nails Irish protector who actually mimicked Liam Neeson's action persona on screen, was leading the charge with another rookie colleague by his side. The club? Absolutely packed, with the kind of madness only London's nightlife can create. Fortunately, our client had a prime corner table, champagne flowing and sparklers lighting up the night, it mimicked those scenes in a wild night club party depicted on the silver screen.

But the real action came when we were posted by the lavatories. As we returned to the table, I noticed two obnoxious men eyeing my client's 'assets', proudly on display for all to see. Instinctively, I knew something would go down, and it did. As they passed, my colleague confirmed they had brushed past her inappropriately, just as I'd anticipated. The fury inside me was palpable. I immediately asked him to check if she wanted them thrown out, but of course, that was easier said than done. I confronted the rude party goer and grabbed him by his arm giving him a good talking-to. The *larger-than-life* Russian bouncers were quick to step in, letting me know those guys were 'big deals' and, of course, I should back off. What a mess.

By this point, my client didn't care about the scumbags, and we made our escape, heading for a midnight breakfast at a 24/7 diner. You see, no VIP experience is complete without a little *grease*. We made sure to *adjust* the staff's attitudes to skip the queue, sparking protests from the other guests. After nearly 22 hours on the clock, I was running on fumes, but this was the reality: the grind, the madness, the adrenaline. Welcome to the life.

Side note: You can't rely solely on assumptions, and things won't always unfold as planned, be prepared to pivot and adapt.

Chocolate Ice Cream Emoji!

Now, I don't want to sound like a whiny little B*tch, and let me make it clear that I'm not complaining. I found myself on the cushiest and bougiest security detail the planet has ever seen, a governmental gig on one of the Caribbean's most drop-dead gorgeous islands. I mean, it was crowned the world's most beautiful beach or island that year. Talk about a tough job, right?

My team were like the Avengers of security details, world-class guys getting along without a hint of ego or a chip on their shoulder. We were practically a security dream team. One fine evening, we played chaperones for a few clients, heading out for dinner and a night on the town. Now, this island was so small; there were only two legitimate options to socialise, either with the locals or the expat community. We even had a cheeky American tourist entertaining thoughts of doing unimaginable things to me while on duty right in front of our clients; naturally, having me blushing. Very appropriate indeed!

As the night aged like fine wine (or tequila, considering the location) and the clients' sobriety plummeted, I received the call to gracefully escort them back home. Now, I can bet my limited-edition sunscreen that no bodyguard on this entire planet has ever heard a response like the one I'm about to spill.

I calmly informed the young female principal that it was time to call it a night, and what did she respond with? Brace yourself for this incoherent masterpiece: 'I'll Sh*t All Over Your Face', complete with giggles for dramatic effect. Now, I'm not sure if this was an actual sexual advance or insult, but I was in no mood to wipe 'chocolate ice cream' from my face! At that time in my career, I had believed that exclusive clients were articulate, polished and composed in their speech, appearance and demeanour. In this instance, I might as well have been outside a pub late at night in Blackpool.

You may think this is hard to believe, but I actually asked her twice, and just to prove it, I've got the voice clip saved to this day as a reminder. Who knew security could be so glamorous? What a class act!

Side note: Staying poised and articulate is no small feat when confronted with the full force of inebriation.

Scandinavian Flick

Setting: I'm on this wild adventure in the Nordics, dreaming of a cosy hotel room after a marathon of a stint. I finally check in, and who welcomes me? None other than a super cute blonde Scandinavian receptionist. Talk about a silver lining on a long, exhausting day. Once I settled in, I hit the gym, took a shower and snuggled into the plush bed, I was ready for lights out. But guess what? My lights came back on, and it wasn't for a surprise serenade by the cute receptionist. No, it was more like a bachelor party extravaganza happening down the corridor. Dream-shattering, right?

Now, instead of basking in the afterglow of my cute receptionist daydreams, I found myself morphing into the hotel detective, fuelled by annoyance. I stormed down the corridor to investigate this unexpected soirée. Imagine this chaotic scene: an open hotel room door, a trashed room, an older, bloodied chap in boxers and a white shirt cowering in the corner, and a topless woman striking a warrior's pose wearing a skimpy thong, ready for action. She looked as if she owned the place and the bizarre scenario.

I yelled at both of them, 'What the hell is going on here? I'm trying to sleep!' The poor chap looked like he was facing the wrath of the century. Turns out, the topless warrior threatened to spill the beans on his shady doctor activities back in England. Drama much? I couldn't take it anymore. I gently (okay, not so gently) grabbed the terrified chap by the scruff of his neck and 'kindly escorted' him out of the room. The African Queen followed suit, still shouting and accusing, jumping and bouncing around with her exposed coconuts and thong. The duo scurried to reception, and I was left feeling like the hero this hotel didn't know it needed. Finally, I crawled back into bed, hoping to pick up where my dreams left off, minus the unexpected topless warrior showdown.

Bonus: I ended up with the receptionist's telephone number, maybe it was out of guilt.

Side note: Sleep is essential in this industry. Prioritise your rest and recovery, whatever it takes, even if it means acting like a hotel bouncer to secure it.

Scandalous

After tackling a Herculean task in Copenhagen, my buddy, who will be referred to as Razor henceforth, and I were practically begging for some well-deserved R&R. Naturally, we thought, 'What better way to unwind than a visit to a local adult entertainment venue?' It was the low season, so the joint was practically our personal playground. And being two rather strapping and handsome lads, Danish Beauties flocked to us faster than you can say 'Carlsberg'.

If my memory serves me right, I had a distracting mix of brunette and redhead (I blame my overwhelmed brain) by my side while Razor scored a stunning blonde. The night kicked off with drinks flowing and desires intensifying. But as things got messier, I had this brilliant idea to switch partners. The ladies were all for it, incredibly hospitable and open-minded.

Then, in the heat of the moment, Razor's newfound friend decided to take a seat on my lap, presenting her perky bosom right in front of my face. Well, being the red-blooded, straight guy that I am, I did what any guy would do in my intoxicated state, I handled and tasted what was on offer. The revelation hit me like a wet fish, her bosom wasn't just bosom; it was wet and slimy. Turns out, I unknowingly dove into Razor's sloppy seconds, and I might as well have made out with him. Horror set in, but hey, we forged an unbreakable bond and hit a new level in our 'friendship'.

A whopping €1800 later, we stumbled our way to the principal's suite and crashed on the settees, nearly missing our early morning flights the next day. Just your typical operator standards, work hard, play even harder.

Side note: Alcohol is a toxin that often leads to unintended actions and lingering regret.

Frozen

One of the most uncomfortable rotations I endured occurred deep in the icy wilderness of Norway. I have a very strong fondness for the Norwegians. I vividly remember being blown away at the sight of three Norwegian beauties at the airport dating back years prior to the plandemic: First, at check-in, where I giggled like a schoolboy and was at a loss for words as I gazed upon the Norwegian blue-eyed beauty checking me in. Second, at the café, another drop-dead beautiful barista solidly caught my attention. And then lastly, at the perfume counter.

Now the issue with close protection is that you are judged and ridiculed if you have to call in sick, especially on a travel detail when everyone is a pivotal asset to ensure the operation functions! So, when I caught a 'cold/flu' from my colleague Hardman, I had to suck it up and hide my symptoms as best as I could; the team leader was adamant not to let the client notice! My worst side effects were the cramps I suffered in my hamstrings; I thought those years of avoiding stretching post-workout were now back to haunt me with great vengeance and thunderous inflicting pain!

I recall setting up a nearby cabin with a fireplace for the client and heating up my hamstrings in order to soothe the awful cramping coupled with using his foam roller, but nothing I did could alleviate the awful pain. Painkillers were the only alleviating comfort. As I stepped out, the Norwegian winter didn't help my crampy hamstrings at all. Moments like this, you just have to suck it up, be brave and look ahead, knowing that this will be over soon and become a mere memory. As it turned out, I contracted Covid from a colleague and that the excruciating cramps I was suffering were not from a lack of stretching and had to soldier on as the saying goes.

Side note: Prioritize stretching and maintaining flexibility for as long as possible. Remember, failing to prepare is preparing to fail. Anticipate a range of possibilities and plan accordingly, because when it comes to uncertainty, you're the one in control.

Paparazzi

Some days in security are routine, and others throw you straight into the action. This was one of those days.

I was assigned, along with a fellow agent, to provide security for a world-famous footballer during a very private commercial shoot. Everything started smoothly, arriving early, securing the location, meeting the crew, nothing out of the ordinary. That is, until we learnt the shoot was happening on a rooftop, surrounded by towering apartment buildings and office complexes. Brilliant! (And by "brilliant," I mean a potential logistical nightmare.)

Soon, our VIP arrived, went through make-up, and then casually prepared to perform aerial acrobatics on the rooftop, dodging vents, pipes, and, of course, the sheer drop to the pavement below. I had to hand it to him, he was fearless and fully committed. Kudos!

While he focused on defying gravity, my partner and I focused on something else: paparazzi. With hundreds of windows overlooking our location, we scanned the skyline for any sneaky photographers trying to cash in on an exclusive shot. Sure enough, someone from the operations team spotted movement, a man with a long lens, perched on a distant rooftop.

Damn, these guys are good. I couldn't help but wonder how much he'd make if he got the shot. Probably a small fortune.

Time to act. With no time to waste, I teamed up with one of the assistants and we made our way to the apartment complex. Once inside, we knocked on the door and were greeted by a pleasant but slightly sheepish tenant. After a quick chat, we turned our attention to the pap, hoping to negotiate. Legally, he was within his rights to stay put and keep shooting, annoying, but true.

So, we switched tactics. Uno reverse card. Instead of trying to move the photographer, we made a better offer to the apartment owner. A little cash incentive later, and just like that, the pap was politely shown the door. Mission accomplished!

With the rooftop secure, the shoot continued without a hitch. Admittedly, the endless re-shoots weren't the most thrilling part of the day, but years later, when I finally saw the finished advertisement, it was worth it. A cool, cinematic masterpiece and we played a part in making it happen. Just another day in the life of a security professional!

Side note: Resourcefulness and strong negotiation skills can take you far in life.

Sex, Drugs & Rock & Roll

This tale is a little on the R18 side, as the title so aptly suggests, to the point. One fine Friday evening, after our detail ended looking after an assortment of protectees, we found ourselves in a secluded bar tucked away in the far reaches of the world. We needed to blow off some steam, so the evening started off with dinner, and then the drinks kept on pouring. I was, luckily, off for the weekend, but my colleague JJ unfortunately had to work, so he took it easy.

Our detail was coming to an end and the contract we had wasn't going to be renewed, so naturally, we enjoyed a little slice of paradise as much as we could. We had an awesome, fun, entertaining evening. Now we were on a very small secluded location and often when we were off we'd run into our colleagues looking after our clients who also quite rightly wanted to socialise. All I recall was running into my client in a rather tipsy state and I saluted him, I mean that's what one does in that state to show respect, right?

Anyway, when it was time to leave, two of the local ladies decided to corner me into their car. I did not want to go alone, so I told JJ that if he were to tag along, I'd work his shift the next day (you will say and do dumb things when you're under the spell of alcohol, a very bad decision, as it turned out to be).

Anyway, we arrived at the ladies' residence. Rock & Roll music was blaring, we were given more drinks, but I felt extremely peckish, so I kindly asked if there was something to eat. The lady, let's refer to her as Vixen, kindly offered to make us both omelettes. The other lady left the get-together, so it was only JJ, myself, and the Vixen. Now, I must stress that at this point in my life and career, I had not once touched drugs, nor even smoked a cigarette. Alcohol was the only poison I knew of introducing into my system. In essence I was a virgin to any sort of mind-altering substances; bear that in mind, so to speak

The Vixen was a skilled chef; moments passed, and our omelettes were ready. But these were no ordinary omelettes, she even took the time to garnish them with 'greens and herbs' that I can only describe as oregano. I was famished, so I gobbled mine up in my drunken state. JJ, however, was reluctant, so I asked if I could have his, which I wolfed down within minutes.

More drinks were passed around, music was on full blast, and then the Vixen decided to dance, but it was no ordinary dance. She was dancing very seductively. JJ and I gave each other a look as if to say, *erm... she's definitely down to frolic,* if you know what I mean, readers otherwise known as DTF, though the 'F' has a rather more crass meaning.

As the dancing continued and got more heated, I started to feel a little funny. Now, this wasn't the alcohol speaking, as I very well knew my capabilities when I'm under the influence. I started wandering around her house, not knowing what the heck was happening; my reality became blurry and, at the same time, I got very, very sleepy. I face-planted onto her leather settee and I was lights out.

During my slumber, I woke momentarily on a few occasions to notice JJ inserting his index finger into the Vixen's lady garden. The next memory I recall was the Vixen, standing naked next to me, grabbing my right hand and playing guitar with her lady bits! That was a first!

As I woke up again, I saw JJ passed out on the floor. I was still heavily dazed and confused. The next thing I knew, the Vixen got on her knees, pulled down my trousers, and started going to town, if you know what I mean, without spelling it out! I was dragged to her bedroom moments later. A few seconds lapsed and I passed out again until I was rudely woken up by JJ. He so gently reminded me that I had offered to cover his shift. I was heavily hungover. I had to rush to my flat, shower, get coffee, and go to work as professionally as possible.

It was only later, with sobriety (and a growing sense of dread), that I realised the truth of what had transpired: I had, in fact, been drugged by weed omelettes and sexually assaulted.

Until that night, it had never crossed my mind that such things could happen to men, yet happen it did, and this tale serves as a sobering reminder to us all. In hindsight, if I had been drug tested, I wonder what may have happened?

Side note: Nefarious intentions can be wrapped up in kindness.

Chapter 5: Opulence

There's no denying that close protection work at the highest level comes with its perks, but let's set the record straight: it's not all glitz and glamour. Behind the luxury is a profession built on discipline, precision, and relentless situational awareness. As bodyguards, we're trained to observe, assess and act, constantly scanning environments, anticipating risks and protecting clients who often expect perfection under pressure. The work is intense, the stakes are high, and true downtime is a rarity. We become masters of problem solving as a priority, making our clients lives much, much easier and seamless.

Yet, when the clients depart and the mission ends, that's when the rewards begin to surface. For those who reach the elite tier of this industry, the experiences are truly extraordinary, private jets, mega-mansions, executive chefs, exotic cars, and access to destinations most only see on screens. But don't be fooled by the celebrity associations. The glamour is often a façade. High-profile clients are demanding, emotionally complex, and rarely predictable. Serving them well requires more than strength, it takes patience, adaptability, and emotional intelligence.

At first, flying on private jets seems like the pinnacle of success. But after enough back-to-back flights with minimal rest, even the luxury loses its lustre. You're not a guest, you're on duty, alert at all times, sleep-deprived and focused. Ironically, I came to prefer commercial Business Class for the chance to enjoy a bit of privacy and genuine rest. That said, the in-flight cuisine is something else, think Alaskan king crab, freshly caught seafood, premium steaks, handmade pastas, and desserts worthy of Michelin stars.

And the lifestyle? It's every bit as breathtaking as it sounds. Palatial residences that feel like movie sets, exotic vehicles that turn heads at every traffic light, and five-star accommodations where excellence is simply the baseline. As someone who appreciates fine food and refined experiences, I've been spoilt. My go-to hotel chain? The Four Seasons, flawless in detail, always exceptional.

This is the reality of life as a top-tier bodyguard. The perks are real, but they're earned, not handed out. It takes grit, long hours, and unwavering commitment. Few get to see this world. But if you're driven enough to reach it, I can assure you, it's worth the climb.

4 Countries 1 Day

The day was a whirlwind of luxury, speed and seamless precision. We departed from a secluded European hideaway, discreetly making our way to a private terminal, where our sleek jet awaited. Our destination? The French Riviera, the epitome of glamour and exclusivity. As we descended towards the tarmac, the view was nothing short of breathtaking, a runway lined with private jets, each more extravagant than the last. *Bienvenue to the playground of the elite.*

Upon landing, a racy SUV awaited, purring at the kerb with one of our colleagues behind the wheel. With the client securely in tow, we effortlessly crossed into Monaco, ticking off our third country of the day. The meeting was brief, mere business formalities – before we whisked him away to the next indulgence: a luxury day yacht, moored and ready at the marina.

The client had only one request before departure: a refreshing dip in the Mediterranean's crystal-clear waters. As the yacht drifted into a secluded, picture-perfect bay, I had no choice but to suit up – channelling my inner David Hasselhoff – and stand watch as the world's most stunning natural infinity pool unfolded around us. The temptation to 'accidentally' fall in was real. The water was a mesmerising shade of blue, inv

But duty called. Soon, we were back on board, racing towards the private jet, where lunch and a seamless departure awaited. Our final destination? A secluded mountain retreat, where the evening ended wrapped in pure serenity beneath a blanket of stars.

Side note: Another day immersed in a world of luxury, velocity and unwavering discretion. Savour each moment, it passes in the blink of an eye.

The Italian Job

We were on the Italian coast during the summer one year in an awesome detail with the VIP. We boated across from the mainland to a very well-known Italian island to get our client to an important meeting on time. This was a closed-off meeting that the team leader and I couldn't attend. We were forced to spend the day lounging in the sun and enjoying the local cuisine while people-watching.

As the day came to a close, we waited for our client near the docks to reach us amongst some super yachts. I started chatting with a Super Yacht rep, and when I managed to get her number, the team leader was impressed and happy. As our client arrived, we escorted him to the little Italian Van with our local driver, who resembled a hairless Mario from the famed video game. 'Mario' was a very short, older local driver whom we hired to escort us through the windy roads on this picturesque little island. The plan was to take a helicopter back to the mainland, but the helicopter was positioned on the opposite side of the island, and we had a cut-off time. Since the meeting ran over, we were in a frantic rush to make the deadline as the pilots mentioned they wouldn't be able to leave past a certain time.

Moments were tense and stressful. It's natural for Bodyguards to take the blame for events beyond our scope! While we were dodging and cornering the twisting narrow roads with the client, out of the blue, we heard a loud notification coming from Mario's phone 'MAIL MOTHER F***ER'. The absurdity was so random that it immediately hit us with snickering laughter, which we tried to contain. Our client simply gave the driver a look without any comment or reaction, which made the whole scenario even funnier. Luckily, we made it to the HLZ on time and were able to share this nugget of humour with the waiting security team on the other end.

Side note: Being forced to suppress one's laughter is the best form of laughing!

City Lights

Paris! The city of love, lights and, apparently, highway robbery disguised as room service. Marky, the executive assistant (let's call her 'EA'), and I had arrived a day early to advance the city for our client's visit. As seasoned professionals, we checked into one of Paris's most prestigious hotels – Le Bristol. And when I say prestigious, I mean four Michelin stars, No. 40 on the world's best hotels list, and a level of luxury that makes one question one's entire financial existence.

As I settled into my suite (*emphasis on suite* – because at these prices, it better have been), I decided to multitask. Why not tackle some report writing *and* sample the world-class room service? Efficiency at its finest! That is, until I opened the menu and promptly choked on my own breath.

A burger – yes, a B-U-R-G-E-R – was north of 70 Euros.
A chocolate milkshake? 20 Euros.
And just for laughs, I skimmed the wine list and nearly fell

off my chair. One bottle priced at a casual 18,000 Euros. For that price, I better gain *immortality* after one sip. But hey, we were living it up. And I had to admit, everything about this place was pristine. The service? Impeccable. The dining experience? Straight out of a black-and-white classic French film. I half expected a young Audrey Hepburn to waltz in, croissant in hand.

Of course, we had work to do, so Marky, EA, and I ventured out to get acquainted with the city. We shopped, marvelled at the Eiffel Tower, and wrapped up the evening with a sublime steak frites dinner at a Parisian institution. No menu, no fuss, just steak, chips and a mystical green sauce that had the entire city queuing into the streets. And let me tell you, it lived up to the hype.

Bright and early, we collected our client from the airport. One of his Parisian routines involved walking meetings in one of the city's immaculately manicured gardens, a genius move, really. Pat and I trailed behind, keeping our eyes peeled, ensuring everything ran smoothly. Eventually, our client signalled, time to head back to the hotel. Simple enough, right? I signalled to our driver, expecting a swift response, a quick pick-up and a seamless transition back to luxury. Nothing.

I tried again. Radio silence. I called her 'phone. No answer. At this point, our client was getting frustrated. I was getting frustrated. And Pat? Well, Pat was watching me lose my mind in real-time. I set off on foot to find her. After navigating a maze of narrow Parisian streets, I spotted the car. And then I saw her. Head tilted back. Mouth wide open. Fully. Asleep. She wasn't just *napping* – she was in REM sleep mode, dreaming of baguettes and berets, completely oblivious to the fact that she was supposed to be working. I damn near broke the window, trying to wake her up.

She jolted awake in complete panic, fumbling with her phone, which, by the way, was OFF – as if she had just been rudely awoken from a 100-year slumber. I had never been more mortified. When we finally scooped up our understandably irritated client, the damage was already done. The embarrassment was palpable. After wrapping up the detail, I made one thing crystal clear:

'We are NEVER using her again'. In security, professionalism isn't just expected, it's non-negotiable. When clients trust you with their safety, there is *zero* room for error and definitely no room for mid-shift power naps. Paris was beautiful. The experience? Unforgettable. But next time, I'm checking to see if my driver has a caffeine IV drip.

Side note: In certain roles, effective communication and simply staying alert can be absolutely critical.

The High Life

During one particular stint with a client, I was catapulted into a world of sheer extravagance, a lifestyle so surreal it now feels like a fever dream. As a bodyguard, I found myself rubbing shoulders with the elite, attending the most opulent events and gaining rare behind-the-scenes access to the inner workings of high society. It was as if I had stepped into a parallel universe where luxury reigned supreme.

Take the Grand National, for example a historic spectacle dripping in wealth, aristocracy and pageantry. You'd think it was all sophistication and champagne toasts . . . until the sun set and the event unravelled into absolute drunken debauchery. High heels snapped, fascinators flew and, let's just say, some of the ladies had serious wardrobe malfunctions, not that my eyes were complaining, but hey, I was on the clock!

Then, there was the high-octane glamour of a Formula 1 race. Roaming freely with an all-access security pass was nothing short of exhilarating. Imagine strolling through the paddocks, weaving between billionaire team owners, A-list celebrities and even royalty. The smell of burning rubber, the deafening roar of the engines and the electrifying atmosphere, it was an adrenaline rush like no other.

Now, Broadway shows in the West End? Not exactly my cup of tea. (Brace yourself for a dad joke.) Let's just say I was *Le Misérable* during the live performance of *Les Misérables*. But what did excite me were the private dinners afterwards, where world-renowned magicians would conjure up jaw-dropping illusions right before our eyes. Mentalists and illusionists toyed with reality, making for an unforgettable experience. Now that, I could get behind!

Of course, it wasn't all glitz and thrills. With shopping-obsessed clients, I often found myself transitioning from 'international man of mystery' to glorified luggage boy. There's an unspoken rule in the security world: carrying clients' belongings is frowned upon, as it hampers our ability to react in a crisis. But, let's be real, refuse and you'd be out of a job faster than you can say 'Louis Vuitton'. On one assignment, my team and I were literally dubbed 'the luggage boys', hauling a mountain of designer bags across the globe. It was a logistical nightmare, but we did it with a smile because, well let's just say the pay cheque made it *very* worth our while.

One thing that always fascinated me was the mystery surrounding private performances by mega bands for ultra-wealthy clients. Was it a favour? A multimillion-pound deal? Who knew? But it was a common occurrence, superstars playing in intimate settings while we stood in the shadows, witnessing history unfold up close. A pretty sweet perk of the job.

And then, the pièce de résistance, food. I am, without a doubt, a self-proclaimed foodie, and Michelin-starred restaurants became my personal playground. These culinary temples, helmed by celebrity chefs, were as welcoming as they were indulgent. The best part? Occasionally, they'd sneak us mere bodyguards, samples of their divine creations. Let me tell you, a bite of that perfection was like tasting heaven itself. Any earnings from this book? You can bet they'll be reinvested straight into these gastronomic wonders!

Side note: Luxury has a way of reshaping your perspective over time, it can seep into your personal life, raising your tastes and dulling your sensitivity to simpler pleasures.

Lavishing

I had the privilege of working for a client whose lifestyle could only be described as a breathtaking display of opulence and indulgence. Money was never a consideration; it was simply a tool for creating an existence beyond imagination. The mansion that could only be compared to a palace, with sprawling grounds, marble floors, and rooms adorned in the finest materials money could buy. The exotic car collection was a sight to behold, each vehicle more stunning than the last, from a sleek Lamborghini to a custom-made Rolls-Royce. The accessories looked like a bona fide luxury department store.

The holidays were nothing short of legendary, always to the most luxurious destinations – islands, five-star resorts, the kinds of places where the elite go to escape their hectic world. Of course, the shopping habits matched this lavish lifestyle, with frequent visits to the world's most exclusive department stores, where no price tag was ever questioned.

The events that were hosted were unparalleled in their extravagance, each one more stunning than the last. Picture intimate dinners accompanied by magicians who would weave their craft to amuse the select few guests. Private concerts featuring world-renowned boy bands serenaded her and her guests under the glittering lights of her personal palace. One birthday bash, in particular, stood out, a star-studded affair with a comedian and a now-infamous rapper in attendance – a man currently embroiled in a series of legal misadventures. For the record, I had the honour of driving the Rolls-Royce that night, so I'll gladly take a pass on any association with the madness that followed or the so called freak offs!

However, as a professional in this world of unimaginable luxury, the allure of these high-profile events was always secondary to our primary mission – to protect, observe and anticipate. While the world celebrated around us, we were ever-watchful, scanning for threats, second-guessing our client's next move to ensure her safety, and staying several steps ahead. The paparazzi, with their incessant cameras and prying lenses, were a constant menace, making it a delicate balance between maintaining our professionalism and managing the chaos that surrounded us. At times, the grandeur of it all was nothing more than a backdrop to the ever-present responsibility of safeguarding those who move in such circles.

Side note: Just when you believe you've seen it all, life will always find a way to show you more.

Luxury

In the field of close protection, only a select few can recount a tale as opulent as the one I am about to unveil. Entrusted with the task of advancing a secluded Mediterranean island, my mission centred around securing a boat for my two esteemed colleagues and myself. Our ultra-distinguished client, set to partake in a meeting aboard a superyacht, requested our presence nearby on a vessel for both accessibility and emergency contingencies. What I anticipated as a simple boat excursion took an unforeseen turn as we discovered our package included not only a skipper but also a dedicated stewardess to attend to our every need.

As our client alighted and we escorted him to the awaiting tender bound for the superyacht, we found ourselves granted the luxury of a mini-holiday just a few hundred metres away. Maintaining our unwavering vigilance, we basked in the warmth of a Mediterranean summer day, cooling off in its pristine waters. With a keen eye on the client and unbroken radio communication, we also revelled in a unique dining experience. Displeased with the superyacht's culinary offerings, a boat arrived, presenting a menu from a local pizza restaurant. After placing an order, the boat departed and returned with a bounty of freshly made pizzas – a culinary escapade by sea, unparalleled.

The night unfolded in our private cabins, mercifully devoid of seasickness. The following day, as the superyacht embarked on a leisurely cruise, we trailed behind, indulging in more swimming and sunbathing. Opportunities of this magnitude are rare, and we seized every moment while upholding the pinnacle of professionalism, delivering protective surveillance to our esteemed client. Such extraordinary escapades are the epitome of the unparalleled luxury that life, at times, graciously bestows upon those entrusted with safeguarding its most eminent figures.

Side note: It's perfectly acceptable to indulge and live it up from time to time, even when it's part of one's professional role.

Italy, Venice, Italy

In the enchanting city of Venice, I found myself immersed in a mission that exuded James Bond's sophistication. The hotel where I held my vigilant post had whispers of its own allure, having hosted the cast of Casino Royale during its illustrious production.

My partner and I comprised a discreet yet formidable two-man detail, safeguarding a distinguished elderly couple celebrating their anniversary in the most opulent manner conceivable. Following an exhaustive advance, complete with a meticulous analysis of the area, we were ready to elevate our presence to match the grandeur of the occasion.

As I clothed myself in a sharp suit and a bow tie, naturally accentuated by the gleam of my Omega Seamaster, we embarked on a journey through Venice's labyrinthine canals. Positioned at the rear of a classic wooden Venetian boat, I kept a vigilant watch while the clients luxuriated in the front. Our passage through the canals was a spectacle in itself, drawing the eyes of onlookers captivated by our impeccable attire and the client's ostentatious diamond necklace, which could have seemingly been on loan from the Queen herself.

Our destination was none other than a resplendent opera house, transformed into a mesmerising setting for the evening's proceedings. The interior, adorned with lavish tables, chandeliers and an abundance of flowers and lights, surpassed even the standards of royalty. The live entertainment proved to be world-class, complemented by a set menu that I was fortunate enough to partake in.

Surreal moments like these affirmed my satisfaction in my chosen profession. As the voyage concluded, our efforts were met with a generous tip, a rare acknowledgement in a world where such gestures are not as commonplace. In the field of

Luxury and world-class security, it was a mission accomplished, leaving memories as unforgettable as the grandeur of Venice itself.

Side note: Seize the opportunity, at least once, to immerse yourself in an evening of true sophistication where you will feel connected to a grand, timeless tradition.

Chapter 6: Clients and Confidentiality

One of the *unreal* perks of elite bodyguarding? If you hang around long enough, and luck decides to grace you with its presence, you might just find yourself guarding your childhood hero, or that one person who shaped your entire worldview. I was one of the lucky few, and let me tell you, it's as wild as it sounds.

When I was given the opportunity to look after one of the greatest and most influential celebrities alive, I kept my composure like a true professional, maintaining maximum coolness and respect every step of the way. But then came the moment I'll never forget, the second I said my goodbyes at the airport and made my way home. That's when it hit me. The *shock and awe* of what had just happened started to sink in.

Now, unfortunately, I'm bound by a Non-Disclosure Agreement (NDA), so I can't drop names. But let's just say this person is a *global icon*. The kind of figure that you can't even fathom standing a few feet away from, let alone protecting. But that's the reality when you reach the top level of this game.

A Hard Lesson

The security industry, where one day you're watching a billionaire sign contracts in a five-star boardroom, and the next, you're sitting in your car outside a mansion, pretending you're in a high-stakes spy film when, in reality, you're just trying to stay awake. Such was my life as I climbed the security ladder, tackling everything from glorified neighbourhood watch gigs to rubbing shoulders with the rich and famous.

I had my fair share of dull assignments, staring at a screen monitoring residential security cameras for hours, babysitting a pile of Nike's latest trainers at a product launch, and even playing sentry duty at a swanky hotel while a billionaire conducted his empire-shaping meetings. But then, there were the *good* gigs, like the time I got to provide security for a well-known boxer or met a basketball legend.

But none of those experiences, not a single one, prepared me for what would become the most unexpectedly challenging detail of my early career, escorting lingerie models through a packed venue.

Yes, you read that right. This was peak security work. My colleagues seethed with jealousy while I tried my best to look as professional as possible. The assignment was simple: escort the stunning models from their dressing room to the stage and stand guard while they showcased the latest in lace and silk. Easy, right? Well, young naïve me wasn't ready for what came next.

As the show began, my colleague and I took our positions at the edge of the stage, ensuring the crowd stayed respectful. But suddenly, I noticed something . . . off. A few of the models were locking eyes with me, sultry, seductive stares that felt *a little too intense for workplace conditions.* Was this part of the act? Was I supposed to stare back? Look away? Play dead?! I froze. And then, biology betrayed me.

The mind may be strong, but the body? The body has its own plans, and let's just say my well-fitted trousers became very . . . uncomfortable. Panic set in. This was *not* the kind of 'rising to the occasion' I had in mind when I joined the security industry. I had to think fast. Reposition. Control. Tame the beast. In one of the most *high-stakes tactical manoeuvres* of my career, I subtly adjusted my situation, strategically securing my predicament behind my belt in what can only be described as a covert biological crisis intervention. Meanwhile, the models kept glancing over, undoubtedly amused by my internal struggle.

I prayed for the show to end. When it was finally time to escort the ladies off-stage, I practically power-walked them back to their dressing room, avoiding eye contact as if my life depended on it. Mission accomplished. Hindsight lesson? Turns out, a couple of the models thought I was cute. Would've been nice if the event co-ordinator had passed that memo to me *before* my body decided to put on a show of its own.

Side note: Biology, you can't fight it.

Ridiculous Wealth

Stepping out of the military and into the private security world was a whirlwind, but nothing – nothing – could have prepared me for this. I landed a gig in Spain, working as part of an elite security team for none other than a wildly wealthy and renowned Middle Eastern Royal Family. The set-up? Unreal. We were handed an apartment, given scooters to zip around town, and stationed at a property so mind-blowingly opulent that it looked like something ripped straight from a billionaire's fever dream.

This place wasn't just a mansion, it was a fortress of extravagance. A state-of-the-art security system blanketed the entire property, with sensors so advanced we could track every movement within the estate (don't worry, no cameras inside, just next-level tech). The garage? Forget your average luxury line-up, this was a supercar shrine, a hypercar Valhalla, a collection so outrageous that even the wildest gearhead fantasies would fall short.

And it wasn't just about cars. This family ran their household like a private kingdom, an army of staff at their beck and call, chefs crafting Michelin-star meals, drivers on standby, personal trainers, assistants, housekeepers, you name it. The sheer scale of their wealth was borderline incomprehensible, so vast, so limitless, that it made reality itself feel different. And yet, I couldn't help but imagine how I'd tweak things as if I had any say in this empire of excess.

Daily life was a non-stop spectacle. Deliveries rolled in like clockwork, groceries, designer shopping hauls and, yes, even cars. The world of the ultra-rich operates on a different plane. Nothing is out of reach. Nothing is impossible. And that's when it hit me: when you can have anything, anytime, where's the thrill? No struggle, no anticipation, just instant gratification. It was luxury on steroids, but was it even exciting any more?

Side note: Having it all isn't the be-all and end-all of life.

Super Stars

I vividly remember my first introduction to one of my earliest clients, although I only looked after her for a day. As a wide-eyed teenager, I had spent countless hours listening to her band, watching their music videos, and now, here I was, standing in the same room as her. Let me tell you, after all those years, she still looked as radiant and flawless as she did on screen. There's no doubt that she must have signed some sort of youth contract with the angels to remain so stunningly youthful!

My task for the day was to accompany the band to a high-profile music show where they were set to perform at a well-known venue. As we arrived, the fans went completely berserk with excitement. Naturally, my job was to ensure they didn't overstep any boundaries. It was exhilarating yet nerve-wracking. Just as I was settling into my role, five young boys arrived on the scene, causing the fans to explode into an even wilder frenzy. I had no idea who they were, but it seemed I now had an even bigger task on my hands.

I quickly coordinated with the event organisers, discussing protocol and procedure to ensure I was positioned correctly in case of an emergency or any unexpected incidents.
Everything was set, and we were in control, well, as much as one could be in the middle of such a spectacle. The backstage area of these events is nothing short of a fiasco; order is more of a suggestion than a reality.

The band took to the stage and performed marvellously. My position at the back allowed me to keep a keen eye on everything and be ready to escort them safely to the green room once they were done. However, to my absolute horror, the plan suddenly changed. Instead of exiting the stage as originally planned, they decided to leave from the opposite end, an area that wasn't connected to my position. Without a second thought, I dashed through the crowd, weaving my way through the intensity to reach them. Just as I was making my way through, a group of young boys stood in my path. I had no time to process who they were, I rushed past, shoulder-checking a blonde lad in the process. 'Sorry, bro!' I shouted over my shoulder, not slowing down for even a moment.

I reached the band just in the nick of time and escorted them safely to the green room. As we walked, the ever-stunning Rita Ora approached and complimented my client on their performance. Later, I discovered the identity of the young boys I had unceremoniously shoulder-checked and brushed past in my mad dash. Turns out, they would go on to become the world-famous One Direction. Oopsie!

Side note: Adapt and overcome.

Fanboy

I was fortunate enough to be entrusted with the safety of children whose parents happened to be close friends with the Ramsays. Yes, *that* Ramsay, the one with the sharp knives and even sharper tongue. As part of this unique assignment, I was lucky enough to dine at one of his iconic restaurants. Thanks to my high-profile clients, the staff graciously offered me a complimentary meal. Naturally, I chose a burger, a dish so perfectly crafted it lived up to every ounce of its well-deserved hype.

One day, my duties took an unexpected turn as I was tasked with dropping off the children at Chef Ramsay's actual home. No, he wasn't there, and no, I didn't get to meet him. But stepping into his stunning abode was an experience in itself. The house was as refined as you'd imagine, a true reflection of his larger-than-life persona. In hindsight, swiping one of his legendary knives as a cheeky souvenir might've made for a fun story, but alas, professionalism prevailed.

These moments are the hidden perks of being a high-end close protection agent. The role often grants access to extraordinary locations and the chance to step into lives that most only see on television. It's not just about protection; it's about embracing the unique opportunities that come with the job.

Side note: Embrace new opportunities!

Twins

Now stories like these don't come by often and are rarer than hen's teeth. As a young teenager, I looked up to this celebrity, but he was so much more than a celebrity; he held so many positions in his life and achieved more than ten men could in their lifetime. He is an icon, a legend of a man, and I had the chance to look after him on a trip to the big city; talk about meeting your heroes. It was a dream come true.

As the VIP disembarked from the private jet, I was immediately in awe of his presence, I remember literally pinching myself to check if I wasn't dreaming. I loved listening to him speak; he had a unique accent, and I was in bodyguard heaven. It goes without saying that he attracted a lot of attention wherever he appeared in public. I had a busy few days keeping onlookers at bay and utilising surrounding security to assist me while out shopping or attending events.

Now, one fine evening our beloved VIP was invited to a very famous casino where iconic ladies dressed as bunnies waited on patrons. It was a quiet evening, and everything was going according to plan, but suddenly, a couple of very beautiful waitresses approached me and asked me if I was the son of my client. 'Why yes, certainly, here, give me your number' is what I should've immediately replied, but the question was so preposterous to me that I immediately laughed it off with a reddening complexion. I was naturally very flattered, and that question made my entire trip.

Once the trip concluded, I shook his hand, and I did what any fanboy thought, *I'll never wash this hand again*. I was proud of my accomplishment and the opportunity to have worked for my role model. Naturally, I can't reveal his identity due to the NDA; but if another opportunity to meet him arises, I'd jump on it

Side note: Meet your heroes; they may surprise you.

Star Struck

Picture this: A whirlwind opportunity catapulted me into the heart of London's bustling scene, entrusted with the protection of one of the world's most gifted, stunning and alluring female artists. A last-minute mission had me escorting her through a frenzied shopping spree in a super-busy department store. As a consummate professional, I maintained my composure while stationed at the entrance after thorough area reconnaissance. When she arrived, an initial bout of starstruck awe gave way to the realisation of perfection personified before me. Yet, duty called. Amidst the short shopping task, she drew the attention of every onlooker, turning the store into a frenzy of fans seeking permission to approach. Thanks to my unmistakable 'DON'T FU** WITH ME' demeanour, they respected my authority.

As the excursion neared its end, the VIP, surrounded by adoring fans, approached the waiting vehicle. In a move that left me utterly stunned, she bid farewell to her assistant and, to my total shock, embraced me, planting kisses on each cheek. This unexpected turn of events marked one of the most epic moments of my career. Eager to share this extraordinary experience, I couldn't wait to report back to my Team Leader. This wasn't just a dream; it was the stuff of every person's fantasy, and unbelievably, it happened to me. It was nothing short of unreal. Trust me, I'd love to reveal and brag who the star is, BUT I'm tied to a damn Non-Disclosure Agreement.

Side note: If your job or career offers nothing to look forward to, it may be time to reconsider your path.

Mr. President

I was briefly assigned to a high-profile billionaire client when a credible threat emerged amidst the high-stakes tension of election year. One morning, our worst fears materialised, graffiti was sprayed right in front of the client's offices. The message was clear: We had our work cut out for us.

My role was to assist in ushering in a new, full-time security team. Some of the agents had already been working with me on prior tasks, but now we were preparing for something much bigger. This particular client was a significant donor to the incoming president and had been vocal in his support for the elect. As tensions escalated, we were quickly called into action. Before we knew it, we were boarding a private jet bound for Washington, D.C., a city teeming with political intrigue and security concerns. Our accommodations? The kind of opulent hotel where presidents and high-ranking politicians stay when in town – the best of the best. The mission? To escort our client safely to a major venue for a key event.

The new security team was eager, rehearsing their plans meticulously. Or so they thought. But when the time came for execution, they fumbled. A classic case of overconfidence and underperformance. They followed the wrong vehicle into the venue, and as they realised their mistake, chaos unfolded. Flabbergasted, they started yelling, 'Where is he?' Completely disoriented, their so-called expertise crumbled under pressure. In a profession where precision is everything, this was a glaring reminder of how quickly things can fall apart when you don't have your ducks in a row and a wakeup call that it doesn't matter how much experience you have or execute all the correct homework, things can and will go very wrong!

Side note: Shit will hit the fan, just clean up afterwards!

Two Birds, One Agent

During my short reign with a particular super-well-known ultra-celebrity family, I had my hands particularly full with the female client who was beyond demanding and looked down upon us. There was no way of pleasing this woman. Even though her public persona does reflect her cold and pretentious nature, she was a thousand times more heinous in private.

One busy morning, I had time to advance a retail shop that 'Her Royal Highness' was imminently going to visit with the children. In this profession, you have to troubleshoot like second nature, especially with this kind of client! Now, the designer shop was right in front of a very busy street, and I had to charm the shop owner into allowing me to park in the cramped basement. Close protection is all about resourcefulness until the spanner gets thrown into the gears. So, there I was, chuffed with myself on a solo detail with Maleficent, keeping watch while she was probably shopping for a black cloak to match her shrivelled heart.

Then, out of nowhere, with no warning, her ultra-famous husband pulled up, parked on the busy street/pavement and asked me to keep an eye out. So now I had the responsibility of car guard and bodyguard to a world-famous family in one of the world's busiest cities! I had to juggle charming the traffic police into not giving a ticket to my client by name-dropping him while simultaneously keeping female fans at bay, so I roped in shop staff to aid me with my tasks!

Shortly after he left, we made our way to a different department store where she went lingerie shopping, of all things. How was I supposed to keep my eye on her and not appear to look like some horny creep? I swear she did that on purpose! In hindsight, I should've licked my lips while staring at her all broodingly!

Side note: Empathy and multitasking will get you far.

Stars

One summer evening, my buddy Greg got the call to take point on a high-profile detail loaded with A-list celebrities.

One of the VIPs? A *mighty* superhero, yep, the kind that saves the world on screen but needs us to handle the real-life drama. The plan was simple: get the superstar squad to their VIP box at the Royal Albert Hall and let them enjoy a world-class concert. Sounds glamorous, right? Not for us. The arrival area was an absolute zoo, with fans and paparazzi buzzing like a hive of caffeinated bees. We hustled the VIPs inside, got them settled, and like the highly trained professionals we are, were left standing in the corridor. No concert for us. *Thrilling.*

As the night wound down, I headed to the loading dock to make sure everything was squared away for a smooth exit. That's when I spotted a problem, paparazzi. And worse? They *recognised me*. Shit. The whole mission was about keeping this visit low-key, and now the press had their eyes on us. Thinking fast, I casually played it off: *'You wouldn't know who the client is, they're unknown'.* Sure, I was clearly working, but that little bit of misdirection gave us some breathing room.

Meanwhile, as the final notes of the concert faded, our entourage took a detour backstage. They wanted to meet the band, and, unsurprisingly, so did half of celebrity London. It was a tight space, a lot of star power, and Greg doing what Greg does best, *physically manoeuvre* a famous UK comedian out of the way to avoid a VIP collision. Smooth, buddy.

Then in the midst of all the madness, fate (or maybe just great positioning) put me in the perfect spot, I introduced our *very* famous female movie star to the band's lead singer. Sparks flew. They ended up dating for a while. Yep, security work comes with the occasional dealings in matchmaking.

Greg took over from there, escorting the crew to some ultra-exclusive nightlife spots. And despite all our efforts to keep things under wraps? The paparazzi still managed to catch them.

Side note: Who knew we'd be responsible for introducing a new celebrity couple!

La La Land

Directly after one particularly raucous New Year's Eve, I found myself boarding a long-haul flight from Europe, bound for none other than the sun-drenched glamour of Los Angeles. My mission? To advance a rather spectacular mansion hidden away in the elusive hills of Beverly together with my trusted colleague, Lenny, and an extraordinarily talented chef who had a penchant for culinary theatrics.

Our task was clear: ensure the residence was thoroughly sussed, stocked and secured before the VIPs' grand arrival. The chef, bless his gourmet soul, was entrusted with sourcing the most mouth-watering ingredients money could buy and, judging by the Whole Foods bill, one might think he was provisioning a royal court rather than a simple household. Eye-watering doesn't even begin to describe it.

Naturally, we were also expected to stock the place with an arsenal of elite snacks and a selection of beverages so refined it could make a sommelier weep. After all, nothing but the best for our incoming dignitaries.

Now, allow me to set the scene: the mansion itself was something plucked straight from a cinematic dream. Think sweeping panoramic views of Los Angeles from every imaginable angle, interiors curated to magazine perfection, and a list of amenities that would leave even a sheikh slightly envious. Multiple levels of opulence awaited us complete with a private gym, an outdoor fireplace that roared against the cool Californian night, a glittering infinity pool, and a fully automated home system that managed everything from the blinds to the Bach playing softly in the marble foyer. Lights, music, doors everything responded with a whispered command.

As for the chef's efforts? Well, he outdid himself. Fresh sushi flown directly from Japan (because, of course, supermarket sashimi simply wouldn't do), rare wines, decadent chocolates you name it. The man had a tall order to fill, and he delivered with Michelin-starred gusto.

When not drowning in culinary extravagance, we were dutifully running our advance work scouting routes, mapping emergency services, and inspecting meeting venues. Diligence, dear reader, is the silent companion of luxury. Then, just as the final preparations clicked into place, it happened: the call every security agent dreams of but scarcely believes. **The trip was cancelled.**

Cue the mental cutaway scene: Homer Simpson punching the air in slow-motion euphoria, triumphant soundtrack blaring in the background. Yes, it was that good. So there we were three men with time suddenly gifted back to us. What to do? Hit the bars? Make an ill-advised pilgrimage to Las Vegas? Perhaps something more decadent, like a dive into the neon-soaked nightlife of Sunset Boulevard?

No, dear readers, our inner children roared louder than our inner scoundrels. We unanimously, gleefully, opted for something far better: **Universal Studios!**

There, amidst the wizardry of Harry Potter, the roaring beasts of Jurassic Park, and even a visit to our spiritual homeland, the Simpsons' Springfield, we had the absolute time of our lives. Grown men, yes, but grinning ear to ear like kids in a sweet shop. Moments like these are the unexpected rewards in this line of work, tiny slivers of joy tucked between days (and nights) of intensity and precision.

Side Note: Hard work often paves the way to reward, but every now and then, luck offers a quiet wink and a knowing nod.

Chapter 7: Fun

The world of close protection – it's not all about serious business and life-or-death situations. Trust me, there's a *ton* of fun to be had when you're out there, making new bonds with your teammates. It's like a big, dysfunctional family on steroids, and believe me, shenanigans *are guaranteed* to ensue. We've all had those moments where the adrenaline is high, the laughter is louder and the memories are made that last a lifetime.

Some of the most memorable experiences come during international trips, especially when you have the luxury of time, the company of trusted colleagues or friends, or even the freedom of flying solo. And when alone, well, modern tools like dating apps can add their own kind of adventure.

Arabian Delight

Myself and my colleague, now a trusted friend and business partner, Mark, had the pleasure of travelling with a client to Doha, Qatar, where they had a routine meeting with some of the royals. And let me tell you, if there's one thing the Middle Eastern elite have mastered, it's the art of extravagant hospitality.

Having spent nearly a year and a half living in the U.A.E., I can unequivocally say that Qatar and the Emirates operate on a level of sophistication and precision that leaves the rest of the world in the dust. These nations don't just function – they flawlessly perform. The streets are pristine, the service is impeccable, and the standard of living is borderline utopian. No homelessness, no visible crime and a sense of order that makes the so-called 'first world' look positively third-class. Everyone is welcome – so long as you respect the culture. And honestly, is that too much to ask?!

But I digress. Upon landing, we were greeted by a welcoming committee and whisked away to the St. Regis Doha, a property so grand that even its chandeliers seem to hang with an air of superiority. This wasn't just a hotel – it was a monument to excess, a masterclass in elegance. That evening, we were escorted to a palatial marble masterpiece, where our client dined in the company of royalty. Mark and I were assigned our own lavishly adorned table and, to our surprise, were served the exact same seven-course meal as the esteemed guests.

Now, the golden rule in this profession? Never overindulge. A bodyguard with a food coma is as useless as a chocolate teapot. But these hosts? They wouldn't take no for an answer. Course after course arrived, each dish a gastronomic masterpiece, and soon we were tipping over the edge of comfort. Full? We had transcended fullness. And then came dessert. The waiters arrived, presenting us with glistening, deep-purple pears, their surfaces catching the candlelight like rare jewels. *Fruit? For dessert?* I thought. How . . . underwhelming.

But oh, how wrong I was. One bite in, and my world turned upside down. Inside those seemingly simple pears were delicate layers of black forest cake – moist, rich and utterly intoxicating. It was a sensory ambush, an irresistible, indulgent revelation. I still dream about it.

The next day, our client departed, leaving myself, Mark and the assistant to enjoy the remnants of our Middle Eastern escapade. And before your minds go gallivanting into scandalous territories – no, there was no ménage à trois. Mark was happily married, and I, well, I probably had a girlfriend somewhere in the world (geography was tricky back then). We rather partook in the wonderful amenities the hotel had to offer before making our way to the stunning airport.

To anyone reading this – go. Experience these magnificent countries first-hand. Qatar. The Emirates. The land where luxury isn't just a lifestyle; it's a birthright. It doesn't matter who you are; you'll be treated like royalty. Thanks to this line of work, I've been exposed to realms of pleasure and indulgence that few will ever see. And hey, someone had to do it!

Side note: Luxury can be intoxicating, it may distort your sense of reality, or inspire you to elevate your standards and ambitions.

Cross Country

One client, a true maestro of cross-country skiing, pursued his passion with such dedication that he insisted we master the sport as well. His vision? That in the face of an emergency, we could seamlessly slip into skis and execute a flawless rescue. And so, off to Canada we went, tasked with conquering the art of cross-country skiing.

In just one week, we transformed from novices stumbling through the snow into proficient skiers, adding yet another remarkable skill to our ever-growing repertoire. But this was only the beginning – our pursuit of pristine, world-class snow took us on an extraordinary journey across the globe. If a country had exceptional snowfall, we found ourselves there, gliding through breathtaking landscapes fit for a cross-country king.

With this adventure came the privilege of indulging in unparalleled luxury. Five-star resorts, grand lodges and the cosiest of ski chalets became our temporary homes. The chalets, in particular, were something out of a dream – roaring fireplaces, bathtubs positioned right at the foot of plush beds and mood lighting that turned the snowy wilderness outside into a scene straight from a fairy tale. The setting was irresistibly romantic, yet duty called, and we remained ever-vigilant, ready to spring into action at a moment's notice.

Room service was another indulgence entirely. No request was too extravagant, and we soon found ourselves dining like royalty. Gold leaf on burgers? Check. Gold flakes in milkshakes? Absolutely. At this rate, I was half-expecting to start producing gold nuggets myself! Our time in the frozen wilderness became so extensive that cold ceased to faze me. Numb fingers, icy winds and endless snowfall became second nature. If anything, I grew to embrace the chill, forging a resilience that would serve me in every challenge that followed.

These experiences, these moments and the sheer generosity of our client left an indelible mark on me. To the man who made it all possible – thank you, Sir. Your vision gave us not just an unforgettable adventure but a lifetime of stories to tell.

Side note: Embrace the cold; it's good for you!

Royalty

In the midst of a high-profile task in a bustling metropolis, my colleague and I found ourselves escorting a Royal VIP and her entourage to a dazzling restaurant at the city's core. While the driver kept vigilant watch outside, the Royals indulged in a lavish dinner. Post-dinner, the party migrated to the lounge, where the evening's festivities continued. Here's where it gets shockingly bizarre.

As a seasoned operative, I couldn't help but notice the presence of impeccably dressed single women scattered around the bar – clearly working girls. Flying solo on this mission, I desperately hoped to avoid any unnecessary attention, given the gravity of my task. But brace yourself for what comes next.

In a plot twist straight out of a surreal universe, the Princess beckons me over and casually inquires about my relationship status. Stunned and utterly flabbergasted, I manage a coy but respectable smile. Hold onto your hats – she promptly disqualifies herself as a potential match (I could have blurted out "not so fast, princess" but professionalism prevailed, unfortunately) and points out someone in the group (another royal?) who might fancy me. Nervously laughing in disbelief at this astonishing turn of events, I express my flattery. If it weren't for the dimly lit bar, my blushing red tomato face would have been on display for all to see. I slowly retreat to my post, still processing the sheer absurdity of the situation whilst the nearby working ladies gaze in my direction. Is this the norm in the crazy world of being a bodyguard? Who would believe this wild tale if I tried to explain it? Welcome to the jaw-dropping, unpredictable escapades of a bodyguard's life!

Side note: Still speechless, (Nothing Happened)

Tokyo

I'm not sure if I manifested this – but maybe I did... let me take you back to 2019. Japan was hosting the Rugby World Cup, and if you know me, you know I'm a *massive* rugby fan. I couldn't stop thinking about it. I had this vision that I was *going* – there was no other option. I convinced myself that my client would have a meeting in Japan, so *of course,* I would be there. It's like I planted that thought in the universe and just let it marinate. And guess what? Out of nowhere, it happened. My client had a meeting scheduled, and the date was set. Boom! There I was, on a private jet heading to Japan, living the dream.

I know, it sounds unreal, but let me tell you, this wasn't the first time manifestation worked its magic. Just a while before, I had this idea stuck in my head that I wanted to do close protection on an island – somewhere tropical, somewhere *beautiful*. Every day, I thought about it, visualised it, and kept it in my mind. Fast forward, and boom again, I get a message on LinkedIn, *'Hey, we're looking for someone to do close protection in the Caribbean'*. And just like that, I was flying to the sun, sand and sea. Manifestation is *wild*.

But let's get back to Japan. My colleague and I were on the jet with the client, feeling pretty great after a good night's sleep. We joked around, and in an attempt to add a touch of glamour to the day, I pulled out a rejuvenating face mask for both of us after our five-star dinner. Yes, I said *face mask*. Why not? The finer things, right?

When we landed, we headed straight to what's now considered one of the best hotels in the world – top fifty, easily. And let me tell you, everything was *first-rate*. The staff, the hotel, the amenities, the cuisine – heck, I had the best sushi of my life there. The gym was state-of-the-art, and the views of the city were so breathtaking that they made me forget I was technically 'working'. It was one of those experiences you never forget. Like, 'pinch me, I'm dreaming' levels of surreal.

Now, here's where the universe went full circle on me. One evening, after hours, I felt like I needed a midnight massage (don't judge; a chap's got to unwind). So, I casually strolled to the corner convenience store to grab some funds from the ATM for the service, and out of absolutely *nowhere*, my childhood rugby hero walks into the store. *You can't make this stuff up.* I couldn't believe it – there he was, right in front of me. Without missing a beat, I walked up, shook his hand and told him I was a huge fan. And get this – I even had a picture with him from when I was a child. Some things in life are just *too wild to explain.*

Side note: Take it from me—visualisation truly works. The clearer, bolder, and more vivid your vision, the more powerful it becomes. See it often, believe in it, and watch it come to life.

Jet Setting

When you're flying solo, you get the chance to meet and even form some *interesting* connections with ultra-attractive flight attendants. There was this one time I had the pleasure of sharing a flight with an extremely cute blonde pilot, and let me tell you, the chemistry in the air was as thick as the jet fuel. Some of these ladies will playfully flirt with you, even if you're not exactly inviting it, which leads to some *awkwardly hilarious* banter with your colleagues.

Of course, we must remember these skyward beauties are just like us – always on the go, chasing the next destination and maybe looking for a bit of fun or connection along the way. It's all part of the high-flying lifestyle.

I found that private flight attendants were the female equivalent to our line of work and would make the perfect partner as we're both globe-trotting at the expense of our employer. I was fortunate enough to date a few flight attendants during my tenure as a CPO, they had the perfect sense of fun, adventure and class and the only reason things ended is when things got too serious, talking about babies, yikes!

Side note: Enjoy your own solitude.

Celebrititties

Embarking on a hilariously awkward journey to Morocco, I found myself in the company of a favourite colleague-turned-friend, Greg, and the impeccable Personal Assistant (PA) who was a wizard at her job. We were living the high life in Business Class, and seated next to me was a woman of, uh, seasoned wisdom (okay, fine, she was a grandma), and she decided to hit on me. WTAF, right? Do I look that old? Am I cougar material? She starts boasting about her real estate empire in London and drops hints about her rejuvenating stem cell therapy plans in Switzerland. My buddy Greg and the PA are stifling giggles, fully aware of the awkwardness unfolding.

Fast forward to our destination, and Grandma extends an invitation to her swanky hotel along with her phone number. GULP! Confidence level: 100. Spoiler alert: I didn't take her up on the offer, I swear!!!

Now, on the eve of the VIP family's arrival, I scouted out the villa in the middle of a desert – a literal oasis. This was the resort where VIPs and celebrities would frequent. Lush greenery, palm trees and a massive lagoon-like pool surrounded the opulent abode. But, hold on, someone's swimming in the VIP's pool! I had to do a double-take to make sure I was in the right place. Turns out, it's a topless woman with a vocal range that could rival Mariah Carey. I awkwardly asserted the private nature of the area, trying to be a gentleman, but my gaze seemed stuck. To add to the madness, we were in a Muslim country, and such antics were definitely a no-go. Ah, the 'perks' of the job – get it?

That evening we had a delectable five-course dinner, Greg sneakily got the PA and myself very tipsy, so much so that I almost stumbled and fell in the pool on my walk to our opulent abode.

Side note: Get out there and create lasting memories— that's what life is truly about. It's time to start living fully, people!

The Library

For this particular detail, I jetted into London to set up at a rather swanky establishment – none other than The Connaught, ranked No 46 of the world's best hotels of 2025. Naturally, I did the usual groundwork: secured a sleek Range Rover as the primary vehicle, meticulously drove every route on the client's itinerary, and familiarised myself with all the nearby emergency services – because preparedness is key, of course.

Then, on the eve of the client's arrival, fate – or perhaps sheer dumb luck – intervened. The trip was abruptly cancelled, and as it happened, my rotation was set to finish right after this detail. This meant that, for once, I had an abundance of unexpected free time. I promptly returned the vehicle and, after a moment of contemplation, thought – well, it would be a shame to let a $18,000-a-night (British sterling equivalent) suite go to waste, wouldn't it?

And this was no ordinary hotel room. No, this was an entire apartment, complete with its own private entrance, a grand library and multiple guest rooms. Naturally, I planned to make the most of my unexpected stay. That evening, I ventured out to a popular Irish bar with some friends to soak up the London nightlife. As luck (or destiny) would have it, I met an exceptionally stunning Irish student who, shall we say, greatly appreciated the luxurious surroundings. I'll let your imagination do the rest.

The following evening, I decided to extend the hospitality and invited a good local friend and his wife over for a cosy movie night – along with my new Irish lady 'friend.' Now, of course, we had to be strategic; room service was out of the question lest any unexpected charges appear on the client's bill. Looking back, it was a rather cheeky move to seize the opportunity, but if nothing else, it makes for a cracking story. After all, how often does one get to casually lounge in a top fifty hotel suite as if it were their own?

Side note: High Risk = High Reward

Chapter 8: Awkward

In this profession, you can bet your bottom dollar that things will happen that will completely knock you off guard – stuff you couldn't plan for if you had a crystal ball and a decade's worth of experience. It's the kind of unpredictable madness that makes you question your life choices but also gives you some of the best stories to tell. And trust me, you'll have some stories. The kind of stories that make your colleagues laugh so hard they snort and then immediately start looking at you like you've just returned from a parallel universe.

These wild, out-of-context moments aren't just for a good laugh, though – they're *character builders*. They test your mettle, your ability to think on your feet and how well you can hold it together when everything's going sideways. It's like the universe throws these curveballs just to see if you're worthy. You know, a kind of 'welcome to the club' rite of passage. And let me tell you, when you've survived these chaotic moments, you've earned your stripes. Or at least earned the right to tell the story – and trust me, you'll want to tell it.

The Super Prank

Picture this: I'm on my second tour in the Middle East, embedded with a badass crew on protective operations, holed up in a base so tiny it makes a studio apartment look like a palace. We're surrounded by massive walls to keep the baddies at bay, and when we're not on duty, we're pumping iron like we're about to grace the Mr. Olympia stage. Everyone's chugging supplements like they're the elixir of life, trying to stay jacked and ready. Word on the street was that big-shot companies back home were sending care packages to us poor, sweaty soldiers. So, genius that I am, I thought, "Why not hit up supplement companies for the good stuff?" We're talking cutting-edge, vein-popping, Hulk-mode pre-workouts. One in particular, Jack3D, was like rocket fuel, heart pounding, eyes laser-focused, still wired hours after your last rep. The rumour was, however, that it was laced with something rather too potent, if you comprehend my implication.

Then, BOOM! I strike gold. Dorian Yates, yes, *the* Dorian Freaking Yates, bodybuilding legend has emailed me back! He's offering to hook me and my buddy up with some top-secret, next-level pre-workout to test. All he wants? Before-and-after pics. Bro, I'm already flexing in my head, ready to be his poster boy. The FedEx package arrives, and we're popping this mystery powder like it's candy, training harder than Rocky in a montage. Months later, I'm shredded, six-pack so chiselled you could grate cheese on it. I'm ready to send Dorian my glamour shots, feeling like a fitness fanatic.

But then, a hellish plot twist. The Captain, our team leader, summons us to the operations room. I am anticipating a pat on the back, perhaps even a medal for bicep curls. Instead, he slaps down a full-colour printout of a *gay magazine cover* with, wait for it, *ME* as the star, flexing in all my glory, with the headline screaming, "Puffs and Their Powders!" My jaw drops to the floor. My soul departs my body. The room erupts in laughter. Turns out, the Captain, that sneaky mastermind, orchestrated the prank of the century. Fake Dorian Yates e-mail? Check. Forged signature? Check. Pre-workout? Freaking *Kool-Aid* in a fancy tub! I fell for it like a chump, hook, line and sinker. That fake magazine cover spread faster than Gossip Girl, making the rounds to every unit in the region. Eighteen years later, I'm still being reminded.

Side note: If something seems too good to be true, well guess what?! Maybe Kool-Aid is all you need as a pre-workout...

R18

Right, where do I even begin with this one? As a bodyguard, you inevitably become close to your client, but in this instance, let's just say things got a little too close for comfort.

It was a completely ordinary day – nothing out of the usual, everything running like clockwork. After a morning workout, my client decided he wanted to hit a spa to cool off. No problem! Within minutes, I had the location locked down and made my way over. For some reason, my team leader found the whole situation hilarious but didn't bother to clue me in. Rookie mistake on my part for not questioning that smirk. I secured two tickets in preparation for my client's arrival, and everything seemed normal – until it wasn't. The moment we walked through the turnstiles, my perception of what I thought was a 'spa' changed drastically. This was no ordinary spa. Oh no, my dear reader, this was a full-fledged Bavarian nudist spa! I should've known.

Panic set in. Immediate, cold-sweat, what-the-heck-have-I-done kind of panic. In an instant, I realised that if I were to truly blend in, I'd have to ditch the uniform and get my meat and two veg on full display – for all to see. And to make matters worse? It was winter. Fantastic. As I escorted my client towards the changing rooms – though what was the point, really? – I found myself wading through a sea of sagging balls, flopping dicks and boobs that had clearly given up on life. There was zero shame in this place. Zero. My client, visibly amused by my horror, turned to me with a smirk and uttered, 'You'd better wait outside'.

Now, did he mean outside in the nudist area, blending in with the masses of liberated flesh? Or did he mean outside at the entrance, fully clothed and preserving what was left of my dignity? I wasn't about to stick around and find out. I bolted for the exit like my life depended on it. And that, my friends, is how I survived my first – and last – experience with a Bavarian nudist spa.

Side note: Get comfortable being uncomfortable!

Royal Dinner

Not many in our line of work can claim they've sat shoulder-to-shoulder with the highest echelon of royalty – and I'm not just talking about a polite nod from afar. I still get goosebumps remembering that dinner, a night so surreal I'd almost swear it belonged in a fever dream. I can't spill all the royal beans (for obvious reasons), but picture this: I was on detail with a good buddy, stepping in for our principal bodyguard who was off enjoying some well-deserved time away. Suddenly, out of the blue, our client, a bona fide member of first-degree royalty, extended an invitation for dinner. And in our world, saying no isn't an option – trust me, the keyboard warriors might be fuming right now, spouting off about protocol, but in this profession, you bend the rules when the stakes are high.

The setting was nothing short of extravagant – a sprawling summer mansion with a massive, circular dining table that looked more like a royal carousel. My friend, a hulking South African dynamo with a presence that could silence a room, accompanied me. We were still reeling, trying to wrap our heads around the sheer audacity of it all.

As we took our places among a sea of illustrious guests and a bevy of elegantly efficient servants, the client arrived fashionably late, a deliberate nod to the timeless art of entrance. Drinks were served, but naturally, we declined the alcohol – we were on duty, after all, and a clear head was as valuable as a royal jewel. The conversation around the table flowed in a language so foreign that we could only nod along in silence, hoping our stoic demeanours would pass for refined.

Then, just as we were beginning to settle into the pomp and circumstance, chaos broke out. Midway through the starters, a guest – suddenly bounded into the room wearing what looked like a kangaroo onesie. Yes, you read that right: a full-blown, hopping marsupial costume. The table erupted in laughter, and I exchanged a bewildered glance with my friend. Were we meant to join in the hilarity, or should we remain the ever-stern, professional guardians of royalty?

Before we could decide, the absurdity escalated further. One of the other guests launched into a tirade, berating one of the waiting staff so harshly that the poor fellow bolted off to the kitchen in tears. The reason? He had only just lost his father and was clearly not in the mood for royal ribbing. It was a bizarre collision of high stakes and human vulnerability that left us all questioning what kind of dinner party this really was.

And just when I thought the night couldn't get any stranger, something was directed at me – a comment so shocking and haunting that, even now, I'm sworn to secrecy. All I can say is that I was relieved when the evening finally drew to a close, and my friend and I practically sprinted back to our hotel, our minds racing with the surreal events we had just witnessed.

In the world of close protection, bizarre moments are par for the course. Whether you're dining with royalty or dodging kangaroo-costumed interludes, one thing's for certain: this line of work never fails to keep you on your toes.

Side note: Work on your poker face.

Revenge

Right, where do I even begin with this absolute circus of a tale? This may sound like fiction, but buckle up, folks, because every bit of it is true. I had just wrapped up a close protection task and decided to head to South Africa for a little 'me time' after my Canadian girlfriend unceremoniously dumped me and left my heart in tatters. Naturally, my first thought was, 'How can I be the bigger person here?' And by 'bigger person', I obviously mean making her so jealous she'd choke on her maple syrup. Pain and heartbreak make you do stupid things, don't they?

So, I did what any heartbroken and irrational adult would do. I downloaded a bunch of dating apps and started swiping through the local talent, determined to find someone who'd help me orchestrate the perfect revenge plan. Surprisingly, I matched with a stunning woman – a full-time architect and part-time model. Jackpot! I spilt the beans about my plan (in hindsight, maybe not my best move), and to my shock, she was totally on board. Game on.

Cue the most over-the-top first date you've ever heard of. I picked her up from work and whisked her away to the V&A Waterfront, where I'd lined up a series of activities that would make Cupid himself roll his eyes. First up, a scenic helicopter ride around Cape Town. Romantic, right? First-date goals achieved. Then, a sunset cruise with champagne, complete with snuggles under a blanket because the Cape breeze was as unforgiving as my ex. Naturally, I documented every moment with pictures designed to scream, 'Look at what you're missing!'

After the cruise, I took her shopping for trainers (because why not?) and then to a steak dinner at one of the best restaurants in town. To top it all off, we rode the Ferris wheel, where she asked to see photos of me with my high-profile clients. I hesitated, but hey, anything for the plan, right? By the end of the evening, I was starting to think, *Maybe this isn't just revenge. Maybe I actually like this girl.*

Fast forward to the next day. I'd booked us a room at the luxurious Twelve Apostles Hotel – a mountain-facing suite, no less. I went all out: a welcome hamper with chocolates, nuts, drinks, as well as a couples massage. I was *so* confident that this was my moment that I sought advice from my friends. They assured me that I was about to 'get lucky'. So, like the over-prepared lunatic I am, I stashed a Durex condom between the mattress and the bed for quick access. Genius, right? Spoiler: No, not genius.

When my date arrived, fresh from a photo shoot, she looked drop-dead gorgeous – sand still clinging to her from the beach. I escorted her to the spa, where she insisted I turn around while she undressed for the massage. Classy, but also not a great sign for my plans. After the massage, we splashed around in the hot pools, and.... . nothing. Zero chemistry, zero physical contact. Just polite conversation. My confidence was slipping faster than a toddler on an ice rink.

And then came the moment of truth. We returned to the room, where the hotel's turn-down service had worked its magic. As we admired the mountain view, she suddenly turned, her voice echoing through the room: 'WHAT THE F***?!' The blood drained from my face and my erection faster than a toddler's inflatable pool popping. There, on the bedside table, was the Durex condom I'd so carefully hidden. The turn-down service had found it and decided, in their infinite wisdom, to place it prominently on display. If I could've melted into the floor, I would've.

I scrambled to distract her with the hamper while I snatched the condom and shoved it out of sight. She didn't say a word, but her face said it all. I mumbled something about giving her space to get ready for dinner and bolted from the room. Mortifying doesn't even begin to cover it.

Dinner was no better. She casually mentioned that she wanted to date a nice Jewish guy. I am not that. By the time we got back to the room, she opted to sleep on the spare bed, likely scarred for life by the whole ordeal. And me? Well, I have a rare sleep disorder where I..... . let's just say I'm not the best bed mate when I'm dreaming. When I woke up, she was still on the other bed, and breakfast couldn't come fast enough.

In the end, I uploaded a photo of us to WhatsApp, deleted her number to avoid looking like a creep, and called it a day. My ex did see the photo and called to yell at me, so technically, the revenge worked. But let's be real: was it worth it? Absolutely not. Lesson learnt: revenge is messy, embarrassing, and almost never worth the hassle. Thanks for the memories, life!

Side note: Revenge is only reserved for small-minded and petty people. Move on and don't look back as karma is a very real solid force to be reckoned with!

Spectacle

One fine sunny day in London (yes, you read that right, it was actually sunny), I escorted my client to a massage appointment (No, it was not a happy ending kind of massage) and took my post outside, scanning and screening the thousands of weekend shoppers. Waiting can be dreadfully boring, so I turned to people-watching to pass the time.

After about thirty minutes, I noticed a short guy in a hooded raincoat striding purposefully down the street, a scowl on his face. As he passed me, he pulled the hood over his head and darted into Specsavers. Mere moments later, he burst out of the store clutching a pair of sunglasses, with two shopkeepers hot on his heels, shouting after him.

It was clear as day that this guy had just pulled a fast one, even though I hadn't seen the actual swipe. Taking a risk, I decided to apprehend the alleged thief. As he sprinted past me, I tried to trip him with my leg, but he vaulted over it like an Olympic hurdler.

Fuelled by adrenaline, I took off after him. I finally caught up with him on a quiet street and demanded that he hand over the stolen goods. At first, he resisted, and we collided like pro wrestlers. But then, realising he was outmatched, he surrendered the sunglasses.

Casually, I strolled back to Specsavers, returned the purloined shades and resumed my post. I checked with the receptionist to confirm my client was still enjoying her treatment and that all was well. Just another day in the life of a bodyguard, mixing crime-fighting with client care!

Now, I will be lambasted by many, many, many security professionals for briefly abandoning my post and leaving the client unsecured. They would be correct; don't do this ever. Learn from this story, and when adrenaline kicks in, do what you must to tame it.

Side note: Do the right thing even when you're not meant to act.

Hell

Not all days go according to plan, and the reason you have a bad day is that you are not prepared! The client in question, or shall I rephrase the devil in disguise, think of her as a more evil Cruella, threw a curveball by not allowing me free time to advance a location that she was due to visit the following day. Now if it was that important to her, she'd have allowed me to do my damn job so it would run smoothly! The she-devil's answer was to 'simply use the GPS'. I did as much route planning as possible and even got advice from colleagues to get me there on time using the best routes.

Right! The next day, we saddled up in the SUV and set off for the rendezvous, which was so important that she even cancelled a trip to the USA! As we were driving, she repeatedly interfered with the GPS, selecting radio stations, which hampered my ability to navigate correctly and effectively and threw me off my game. She eventually stopped the navigational torture and switched it back. Time was running out to get to the location on time. As we were nearing the turn-off, I misread the GPS and turned instead of remaining straight, which would eventually have led to the turn-off. The GPS recalculated, I held my breath, my sphincter was overworking, sweat was starting to bead on my forehead, and it added 30 minutes. . . FUUUUUUUUUUUCK! She didn't notice; at this point the front windows were misting up from my perspiration. We were definitely missing the event!

I built up the courage to let her down gently. . clearing my throat, I let her know there must've been a 'glitch' (white lie) with the GPS, and it's added 30 minutes. . . ALL HELL BREAKS LOOSE, appropriate for her as she is evil personified!

I don't recall a word of what was said, but shouting and screaming ensued. I failed. I felt like the world could open up and just swallow me whole! The guilt I felt was unfathomable; I was apologetic as can be, trying to remain professional. She started crying hysterically. I kindly offered a packet of Kleenex, and she swiped them, blew her nose and threw her snot rag at me. Guess I deserved that. I tried to soften the blow, stating that I'd remove myself from the detail as punishment!

The theatrics continued, the shame is palpable and intense, my fists clenched the steering wheel trying to alleviate this thick burden, I **nearly** broke and yell, 'IF YOU ONLY LET ME FU**ING DO MY JOB, THIS WOULD'NT HAVE HAPPENED, YOU FU**ING C*NT'.

At this point, I was contemplating stopping the car on the motorway and simply walking home. Anything would be better than the verbal abuse I was suffering! The witch expected me to drive and call her contact at the event to let them know of our late arrival, so in essence, breaking the law and running the risk of losing my licence if caught by the ever-vigilant police. I guess it was part of her revenge plan.

Upon our arrival, I was as contrite as possible to her companion. She swiftly departed with her partner and entourage, leaving me behind to take another car back to the city.

In all dead seriousness and complete honesty, when I finally left that detail, it literally took me years to stop having nightmares from living and working with that demonic woman! I wouldn't wish that experience on my enemies!

Side note: You will come across demonic people in your life; don't allow them to affect your sovereign sanctity of reality.

Little Monsters

One of my more unique assignments was escorting two young ladies to a Lady Gaga concert. One of them from a royal bloodline, which immediately elevated the stakes. My task? Develop a seamless logistical plan for navigating a massive venue, ensuring safe and timely entry and exit. The challenge? I had no opportunity to conduct an advance visit – no chance to scout the venue or test routes in person. Instead, I relied entirely on online research and Google Maps to plan our journey, which, of all things, involved arriving by train. Let me tell you, as someone accustomed to having control over every detail, this was far from ideal.

To make matters worse, I had never been to the venue before. Fortunately, we had an ally: a member of the star's security team who promised us expedited access to the front row. That sounded great – until I realised we'd be smack in the middle of Lady Gaga's most devoted fans. Now, I had no idea what to expect, let alone how those fans would dress, but I quickly found out.

Everything was going smoothly until we approached the stage. It was like stepping into a surreal Halloween party with hundreds of kids and adults in the most eccentric outfits I'd ever seen. Meanwhile, there I was: 6'5", towering over everyone, dressed in business casual as any professional agent would be. In hindsight, a Captain America costume might have been a better choice – I'd have blended in better and felt less like a corporate dad who wandered into the wrong party.

I stood out like a lighthouse among a sea of elaborately dressed 'monsters', as Lady Gaga affectionately calls her fans. No joke, during the performance, Lady Gaga herself glanced in my direction with what can only be described as a mix of concern and curiosity. It was as if she were wondering why a very properly dressed serial killer had made it to the front row. And that, my friends, sums up the unpredictable joys of close protection.

Side note: In hindsight I wish I had a cross necklace around my neck to ward off her stare.

Swiss Shenanigans

One cloudy day near Zurich, my colleague and I took the lift to the basement, where the VIP vehicle was located, in anticipation of our imminent departure. At the time, I was on a very healthy, high-protein diet, and the result of that was windy side effects. As we walked through the car park, I quickly scanned the area and released the hurricane that was built up inside me. In embarrassment, I went to hide behind the SUV in case someone heard a thunderous roar echoing throughout the concrete basement. My colleague, who is an older silver fox from New York, let's call him Lenny, was trailing behind me and in stitches with laughter. At that precise moment, one of the executives who was in the client's entourage entered the car park. She was struggling with bags, so my colleague, who is naturally a very friendly gentleman, ran over to assist her while he was in fits of laughter. She, however, probably did not want him near her as she thought he had a severe stomach upset due to the thunder she just overheard coming from his vicinity (I was still hiding at this point). As I witnessed this, I was bent over on the floor, giggling like a schoolboy close to the point of nearly wetting myself. She eventually drove off with her driver to the next meeting point; meanwhile, Lenny and I were in hysterics that I somehow betrayed him with my high-protein diet.

On our vehicle move to the next location, the executive being in earshot of Lenny and me, I couldn't help myself, and I made sure to ask him out loud, 'How's your stomach feeling, Lenny'. The executive clearly giggled once she heard my traitorous 'concerning' question to Lenny. I got away with the perfect crime.

Side note: Triple-check that the coast is clear, and maybe lay off the extra protein during working hours.

Watch Paint Dry

The most mind-numbingly tedious assignment I ever had was with a residential protection team in London. The client, who has since passed away from natural causes, had left us behind as an insurance policy – mainly because a painting displayed in his entrance foyer was so valuable that insurance companies wouldn't touch it with a ten-foot pole. So, there we were.

Our shift was a gruelling 12 hours long, split evenly between watching over the operations room and guarding the art in the foyer. That meant six hours of our day were spent simply walking around and staring at the artwork. Yes, you read that correctly – walking, standing and observing. There were no chairs to sit on, no moments to relax, just endless vigilance to ensure that the ancient painting, along with a collection of equally bizarre pieces, remained exactly where it was. It was as if we were hired to prove that standing still for hours can indeed be a full-time job. I sometimes wondered if stacking shelves might have been a more fulfilling endeavour.

To add to the misery, we were paid a mere £150 per day. We had to figure out our own transport to the job, arrange our own meals, and then, as if that weren't enough, hand over our hard-earned cash to taxes and National Insurance. The end result was that there wasn't much left to spare. Looking back, I can't help but think I'd have been far better off in a bustling war zone, staying active and, perhaps, even feeling like I was making a difference. In the end, this gig was an exercise in enduring boredom – a stark reminder that sometimes, the most unremarkable tasks are the ones you're forced to do. Never again.

Side note: Be grateful for what you have. If you're not, then visualise your perfect life and strive for greatness.

ANYONE has the ability to change their reality, even you who's reading this right now!

Shivering Sweden

The great pandemic-era misadventure to Stockholm – proof that even the best-laid plans can be derailed by a delayed PCR test and a twisted sense of humour from the travel gods. My buddy and I, full of anticipation for our Scandinavian escapade, approached customs like two seasoned adventurers ready to conquer the Arctic. But instead of adventure, we got bureaucracy. Turns out, our PCR tests were as reliable as a fortune cookie's promise of good luck – they'd expired. Yes, expire Mid-flight. Because apparently, viruses follow time zones now.

Cue the customs officials, who seemed to relish our misfortune with the glee of reality TV judges eliminating hopeful contestants. We were promptly escorted to what was described as 'temporary accommodations', which, spoiler alert, was less cosy retreat and more military barracks with a hint of winter chill.

Snow fell outside as we settled in for what I can only describe as the least glamorous sleepover of my life. The 'beds' were straight out of a boot camp catalogue, and the heating was, shall we say, aspirational. Resourceful as ever, I channelled my inner MacGyver and fashioned a blanket out of curtains, a move that screamed both ingenuity and desperation. My buddy, meanwhile, discovered the joys of vending machine dining – a gourmet feast of pre-packaged misery.

But in this storm, there were silver linings. A sympathetic policeman took pity on us and escorted me to the terminal's functioning area, where proper food awaited. Compared to our makeshift camp, it was a five-star dining experience. And just as we started questioning our life choices, Lady Luck threw us a bone: Bitcoin. Yes, our investments decided to skyrocket mid-ordeal, leaving us stranded but richer.

Not that it mattered to our client, who had reached the end of their patience. They cancelled the trip, leaving us to navigate the labyrinth of Swedish testing protocols one final time. By the time we boarded a private jet to escape this Nordic nightmare, I'd learnt three things: first, never trust a PCR test; second, vending machines are not Michelin-approved; and third, if you're going to get stranded, aim for Dubai – because if you're going to suffer, you might as well do it in luxury.

So, there we were, flying away from Stockholm with snow on the ground and a story for the ages. Sweden may not have rolled out the red carpet, but it certainly delivered the laughs. Next time, though, I'm packing my own blanket – and maybe a backup PCR test, just in case.

Side note: Doesn't matter how much you think you prepare, life will throw you a curveball, take it as a lesson, whatever happen will pass, may as well turn it into a fun story.

Sprinklers Activate

It was a fine evening in jolly old London, and there I was, assigned to protect and serve, well, mostly just drive around a fancy client to various watering holes and eateries with their posh pals. Now, any seasoned bodyguard knows the importance of strategic bladder management. So, before embarking on this adventure, I made sure my bladder was as empty as my wallet after paying London rent. But lo and behold, as soon as I settled into the vehicle awaiting the esteemed client, my bladder decided to stage a rebellion of its own! It filled up faster than a balloon at a birthday party, the treacherous traitor! Hours passed, and with every stop, my desperation grew. I scoured the surroundings for any possible relief – parks, bushes, alleyways – anything to hide my imminent leakage! But alas, we were in the poshest part of London, where even the pigeons wore top hats and monocles, and there wasn't a decent pee spot in sight.

As the pain reached excruciating levels, I resorted to desperate measures. I contemplated using empty bottles, but the thought of explaining myself to the Queen's Guard was enough to deter me. Finally, unable to bear it any longer, I mustered the courage to text the client for a brief intermission. I zoomed past them, my eyes locked on the nearest lavatory like a man possessed. But just as I was about to reach sweet relief, my bladder decided to play its final, cruel joke. It began its own version of the 'Running of the Bulls', with me as the hapless matador. I burst through the bathroom door like a man possessed, my zipper already down in anticipation.

And then, it happened. My bladder, akin to a broken sprinkler on steroids, unleashed a golden torrent in all directions. If anyone had been unfortunate enough to be standing nearby, they would've received an unexpected golden shower. It was a symphony of relief, pain and humiliation all at once. Even when I thought it was over and done with, my bladder had other plans. It was like trying to stop a runaway train with a feather duster – I just couldn't. Lesson learnt: we may be tough bodyguards, but we're still human. Take care of your bodily needs, folks, or risk becoming a walking fountain of embarrassment.

Side note: No point holding it in, just go!

Adrenaline Shopping

Whilst out in London, preparing for the grand arrival of an heiress eager to indulge in some high-end retail therapy on swanky Sloane Street, I spotted a moped with two rather shady characters zooming onto the kerb just two stores down.

They rammed straight into a jewellery store, now an AP Watch Dealership. The security screens shot up immediately, but our moped miscreants were armed with a sledgehammer and some long, menacing weapon, hacking away at the screen door as if auditioning for a villain role in a heist film.

With nerves of steel, I quickly informed the team leader of the situation, recommending we halt the heiress's arrival. But our heiress? She was unflappable. Insisting on her shopping spree, she practically said, 'Let them eat cake!" Dashed to the mayhem two doors down, showcasing immense trust in our close protection skills.

Now, as a protector, I couldn't just stand there twiddling my thumbs. Armed with my trusty umbrella on this rainy day, I channelled my inner Jason Bourne and flung my fancy umbrella at the robbers, hoping to discombobulate them. At that very moment, a police car rounded the corner, and the would-be thieves scattered like startled pigeons.

I coolly returned to my position just in time to welcome the heiress, who breezed into her shopping excursion as if nothing had happened. Truly, it was a day for the books – and perhaps, a future comedy sketch!

Side note: Surprises will happen. Face them courageously. Be fearless!

Close Call

In the world of private security, you meet all kinds of professionals. Some are voracious readers, devouring every book on threat mitigation and hostile surveillance. Others obsess over geopolitical movements like they're playing chess with world leaders. And then you have those who are training junkies, certifications galore, always hunting that next tactical edge. And then... there are the weird ones. The hybrids. People like me.

I like to dabble in everything, knowledge is power, right? But one particular skill really grabbed my attention: lock picking. More specifically? Handcuff escape techniques. (Don't get kinky on me—this is strictly professional... mostly.)

Now, file that away in your brain. It'll be important in about fifteen seconds. So, there I am, flying commercial into a charming little town in France, a straightforward gig. The mission? Advance a key business meeting for a billionaire client. After that, make our way to the private terminal and jet off to the next country. Simple. Smooth. Surgical.

Everything went like clockwork. The client crushed the meeting, spirits were high, and we headed to the private terminal to board the jet. I could practically smell the fillet steak I was about to devour.

And then, bam! French Customs. Now listen, I've dealt with border security from Mauritius to Tokyo, and these French officers were *not* playing around. Bags went through the X-ray with all the intensity of a nuclear audit. And then, disaster. A customs officer with the cold efficiency of a Bond villain pulls me aside, opens my bag... and triumphantly lifts out my set of handcuffs. Cue record scratch. Freeze frame.

Yup, that's me. You're probably wondering how I got into this situation. Behind me: My billionaire client, his assistant, and my colleague, all now watching this unfold like it's some reality TV show.
In front of me: A very unimpressed French customs officer holding up my cuffs like they were contraband at a drug bust.

I asked (calmly, I swear), "What's the problem?" She responded, "This is a weapon. Strictly prohibited." Excuse me? A weapon?! I was mentally preparing for a full-blown arrest scene. Visions of tiny French jail cells started dancing through my head. And my client? Oh, he was loving it. Instead of hopping on his jet, he sat down and watched with amusement, as if to say:

> "Let's see how this bodyguard Houdini's his way out of *this* mess."

Thankfully, I stayed cool. I negotiated that they could confiscate the cuffs—fine, take 'em, I've got five more at home anyway. Then I played my ace card: I reached into my wallet and pulled out my old Police Warrant Card from my days as a sworn Special Constable in a far-off, very real, very tiny country.

She looked at it, paused for what felt like a week, and finally let me off with a stern warning. Crisis averted. No handcuffs, no jail, no international headlines. We got on the airport bus, and for the first 60 seconds it was dead silent. Then my client and his assistant burst out laughing. Because that could've gone *so* much worse. Their laughter hit me like an avalanche of relief.

Special Side note: Always know the local laws, especially when packing handcuffs.

Chapter 9: Relationships

As protectors, we're entrusted with guarding some of the world's most beautiful, fascinating and iconic celebrities. It's a job that requires skill, discretion and a certain level of, well, *coolness*. But here's where it gets interesting – imagine being on a protection detail for someone who's just posed for a tasteful nude magazine. Now, how do you look them in the eye after that? Seriously, how? You can't help but chuckle to yourself and think, *'Well, this has just got rather awkward.'* Yet, somehow, we *do* it. We stay professional because that's what we do best. It's a level of self-control that sometimes makes us seem a little robotic. Not sure if that's a compliment or not, but hey, we'll take it.

But let's be real – sometimes, being this close to such an intriguing world can lead to some *interesting* dynamics. There are moments when protectors get a little too close to their clients, and yes, it's one of those situations you've seen play out in the news. Those agents – sometimes, it's hard to stay mad at them. They achieve the impossible, making the unthinkable happen to protect their clients, but sometimes, their emotions blur the lines. And, let's face it, it's almost always their career that takes the hit. It's a tough pill to swallow when feelings get in the way of professionalism.

But here's the flip side: for those of us who are single and find ourselves with some free time on the job, well, let's just say we have a *lot* of fun. We're not just bodyguards; we're knights in shining armour on a mission to protect and serve with strength, charisma and a whole lot of charm. And what woman doesn't find that irresistible? When you're the kind of protector who carries himself with the quiet confidence of a knight? I'd have done the readers a disservice if I didn't include a chapter on our relationships, you're welcome.

Caribbean Cruising

Imagine this extraordinary Caribbean escapade: After an invigorating close protection detail, my colleagues and I decided to spice up our evening with a dinner outing. Amidst a comical mix-up, a dash of road rage and a disrupted plan, the night seemed doomed before it even began. Unfazed, I seized the moment and steered the car towards our favourite American Burger Spot. However, a mysterious force led me to a fish restaurant right across the street. Upon entering, my eyes locked onto three mesmerising young women at the counter, savouring their meals. Intent on a solo takeaway, I inadvertently drew their attention, sparking a lively conversation.

Instead of a solitary meal, I found myself dining with these enchanting ladies, sharing invaluable local insights about the island's hidden gems. As fate would have it, we left simultaneously, and I gallantly offered to chauffeur them to their accommodation. However, their adventurous spirits had other plans – a spontaneous decision to go night swimming. Ever the accommodating gentleman, I whisked them away to the ultimate night swim spot. Here's the jaw-dropper: we all ended up skinny dipping in the Caribbean under the moonlight. It felt like a surreal experience, and if I could go back and tell my younger self, I'd advise better preparation for such magical moments!

The warm Caribbean waters played host to unforgettable views, and let's just say, I had to extend my time in the water for calming purposes. The remainder of our stay on the island became a whirlwind of shared moments, and, to culminate it, a romantic fling blossomed with one of the lovely ladies. Life truly is nothing less than amazing.

Side note: Opportunity and possibility can literally be around the corner. Get out, socialise, meet people – you never know what friends you can make!

Take Away Love

As a bodyguard, our work often entails long hours, frequent absences from home, and a way of life that doesn't lend itself well to stable romantic relationships. To be honest, there's a unique allure in being a protector, and during my travels, I've encountered many captivating, if momentary, romantic interests. There's an unspoken connection in these brief encounters. They recognised who we were, and we certainly recognised them. It was always short-lived but enjoyable – a flicker of warmth amidst a Spartan profession. These moments were transient, providing a bit of solace in the madness of airports, hotels and high-pressure situations. However, this lifestyle is not particularly suited for the typical married man. Unless you have a rock-solid relationship and a partner who comprehends the long-term picture, it can be challenging. Patience, trust and a focus on the future are essential. Otherwise, being single has its benefits.

Side note: Living a single nomadic life is not fulfilling – find that one special person with whom you can share your life with. We're meant to be with someone!

Playmate - Illustrated

You simply won't believe this next story – it's the kind of tale that sounds too absurd to be true, but I assure you, it happened. There I was, in paradise, enjoying some rare downtime with my team. News reached us that a high-profile magazine photo shoot was taking place on the very same small island we were confined to. You can imagine the stir it caused – models, photographers and whispers of glamour in the middle of nowhere. For a team of adrenaline junkies like us, it was as if the universe had dropped a plot twist into our otherwise routine island life.

That evening, we hit up the only bar-slash-club on the island – a ramshackle spot with questionable lighting and overpriced cocktails. But who cared? The buzz was electric. And then, as if scripted by Hollywood itself, in walked several Playboy Playmates as it turned out, flanked by their hulking security detail. The atmosphere shifted instantly, like the opening scene of a high-stakes comedy.

Now, as I mentioned in the last story, I was 'loosely' seeing an island girl at the time. Nothing serious, mind you, but serious enough to make what happened next a bit complicated. Enter my hilariously cocky mate from Manchester – let's call him Chaddie. Chaddie, never one to shy away from a social challenge, swaggered over to the models with the kind of confidence that only a Mancunian with a pint in hand can muster. To my surprise, he actually got their attention. Moments later, he waved me over, grinning like the Cheshire Cat.

What could I do? I walked over, trying to play it cool, and Chaddie introduced me to one of the girls – a striking woman with an edge of toughness. Turns out, she was a former Air Force soldier. Before I could even process that revelation, she started playfully punching my arm and laughing, declaring that I vaguely resembled Rob Gronkowski, her favourite football player. In that moment, two thoughts hit me simultaneously: One, our kids will be beautiful, we'll have a grand wedding. Two, I am definitely single now.

I wish I could tell you I handled the situation with grace, but, well, I didn't. In a move that still makes me cringe to this day, I decided to make things 'official' with the island girl – by officially ending it. I awkwardly approached her and unceremoniously declared us both single. Yes, I know. Shocking, mortifying and utterly juvenile. Trust me, I'm as embarrassed writing this as you are reading it.

Back at the bar, I resumed my conversation with the model. Things seemed to be going well – she even gave me her number, and we made vague plans to meet later. But the universe, ever the master of poetic justice, had other plans. As it turned out, she was under a strict curfew, and her security detail – built like a human tank – wasn't about to let any late-night rendezvous happen on his watch. And so, my grand adventure ended exactly as it should have – with a giant 'not tonight, old bean' from fate.

Looking back, I can't help but laugh at the sheer absurdity of it all. From paradise to public humiliation, with a dash of Gronkowski and a side of poetic justice, it was a night to remember – and a lesson I'll never forget.

Side note: Simply remain humble and grounded. Realise that your actions impact and affect other people!

Reprehensible

This is the perfect example of how not to have it. There's one detail that still boils my blood to this day. A shameless excuse of a team leader – unprofessional, incompetent and utterly undeserving of his position. For the sake of this segment, let's call him Shameless because that's exactly what he was.

This was the detail leader, the one who was supposed to set the standard. Instead? He was trailing behind the client with his AirPods in, listening to bloody audiobooks. Unbelievable. Worse still? He'd catch a nap in the back of the vehicle – directly behind the client – when we were supposed to be on high alert. I'd nudge him, trying to shake him awake, and he'd give me the kind of death stare that said, 'How dare you interrupt my nap?' Are you kidding me?!

At one point, I'd had enough. I refused to kiss his arse, and naturally, that made me a problem. Soon enough, whispers started circulating that Shameless and his sidekick, the executive assistant – let's call her Traitor – were looking to get me sacked. Next thing I knew, I was being flown to one of the executive's hometowns for a 'stern talking-to' because I wasn't playing along with his bullshit. I wasn't having any of it.

Then, the truth started to unravel. It became blatantly obvious that Shameless and Traitor were sleeping together. Every time we wrapped up a detail, they'd mysteriously linger behind. When he wasn't on duty, he'd fly in just to see her. The over-the-top friendliness, the whispered conversations – it was right in front of everyone's eyes, yet my colleagues couldn't see it!

Then, came the moment of reckoning. We were preparing to depart for Europe, and everything was in place – except Traitor was nowhere to be found. Strange. Highly irregular behaviour, especially given the circumstances. Shameless was supposed to drive the client to the airport, yet as I was waiting on the plane with the luggage, in walks the CFO. Now, this was completely out of the ordinary. My gut told me something was deeply wrong. Moments later, the client and my colleague boarded – but Shameless? Nowhere to be seen.

Just then, the bombshell dropped. It turned out Shameless and Traitor weren't just having a fling – there was money involved. She'd been dipping her hands in the client's proverbial cookie jar, and guess who was helping her cover it up? That's right – Shameless. I vividly recall how she bragged that her wardrobe was probably worth north of a million pounds! Suddenly, it all made sense. The suspiciously low petty cash every time I took stock. The secretive meetings. The whispered exchanges. They weren't just betraying the company; they were betraying the client who had put his absolute trust in them.

The repercussions? Devastating. The entire team was nearly sacked. One team member did get sacked. Another was internally transferred to a different department as damage control. And Shameless and Traitor? They should have been in jail. I still feel for the client. He trusted these two, and they spat all over that trust in the worst possible way. Disgraceful.

Side note: Your gut never lies. If something feels off, it usually is. Loyalty is everything in this line of work. If someone starts getting too comfortable abusing trust, taking shortcuts, or cosying up in ways they shouldn't – call it out. Truth will prevail.

The One

During the year 2020, which is now widely known as the 'PLANdemic', I was locked down with my principal and team at his ranch in the north of the USA. Due to the limited security work, I was handpicked to be the replacement chef for nearly four months; yes, that's right, me, the bodyguard, doing chef work and shopping on a daily basis. Those Gordon Ramsay binge-watching programmes finally came in handy, as did keenly observing my mother cooking over the years.

As time began to stand still, and I began to feel like Bill Murray in *Groundhog Day*, I decided that I needed extracurricular activities, so I resolved to see if I could make a pen pal on a dating application recommended to me by an old girlfriend (a friend who's a girl)!

Believe me, there were slim pickings in the north, close to the border of Canada. But one faithful evening, the application glitched, and the radius expanded to Montreal as the app ran out of decent women in the area. Thank God it did because I was matched with the most jaw-droppingly beautiful blue-eyed, blonde-haired Goddess. Today, without a shadow of a doubt, I would have guessed that she was AI-generated, absolutely flawless. Who would've guessed my dream woman was hiding in Montreal!

We hit it off straight away; we spoke, video-called and messaged each other every waking second for months. We couldn't get enough of each other, so I came up with the idea of sneaking away from work and meeting her at the border. If there's a will, there's a way!

So, we did just that. I drove up directly to the USA/Canada border, parked up short and walked directly up to the Canadian customs. Bear in mind that the U.S. Customs must have been asleep because I mistakenly walked directly over the border into Canada. The big customs lady got such a fright that she blurted out that I'd need to be quarantined. I reversed quickly and walked back. At this point, a U.S. Customs agent approached me, and I haphazardly responded, 'I didn't cross the border' before getting in the car and driving to the correct border point where my Queen was waiting.

Now the rules were that we couldn't cross the border or touch each other, even though that's all we wanted to do! Three metres of exquisite, intense and magnetic atmosphere were separating us. We were infatuated with each other. I asked her out on the spot to be my girlfriend right there and then, with an invisible border keeping us at bay and the border agents keeping a watchful eye on us. A mere seven months later, we were happily married, and have since travelled the world together, creating memories that would make for quite the fairytale.

Side note: The right person is out there for you, even though you never thought it possible.

Closing

A Life Less Ordinary

Throughout this insane journey, I've had the privilege of working alongside legendary clients, elite instructors, razor-sharp team leaders, and some of the best colleagues the industry has to offer, past and present. I have forged lifelong friendships, been mentored by the finest, and had doors opened to opportunities that most can only dream of. I have witnessed the best and worst of humanity, navigated the chaos and emerged wiser, tougher and forever transformed. I am grateful for it all.

Craig, you are sorely missed. Your passing has left a tremendous void in people's lives. I thank you, brother, for everything, for your friendship, your guidance, and the unwavering support you gave me over the years. Without you, I would not have experienced such a colourful and fulfilling career, nor found the motivation to put pen to paper and write this memoir. This is as much your story as it is mine.

I would like to convey my sincere gratitude to a certain distinguished friend and colleague who has generously conferred upon me not one but two eminent roles within this most exclusive industry. Thank you, Dragon, I appreciate you more than you shall ever comprehend. Opportunities like that are rarer than a billionaire flying commercial, and I'll never take them for granted. Pay it forward – always.

I would like to pay heartfelt tribute to two Sergeant Majors who have been guiding forces throughout my journey. Their mentorship and example have left a lasting impact on both my personal and professional life.

I am also deeply grateful to the many colleagues and friends who have shared in this path, too numerous to name individually, and whose names I have chosen to omit here for privacy and obvious reasons.

To those I've mentioned throughout the book: Frances Fox, Hand Grenade, Zim, The Back, Mac Attack, Hardman, and to all my comrades from across the globe, English, Scottish, Irish, American, Norwegian, South African, and many more, I thank you sincerely. Each of you has left an impression on my life, and the memories we've created together will always stay with me. Thank you for being a part of the journey.

Immersing myself in the realm of celebrity and billionaire clients has been nothing short of eye-opening and utterly surreal. Yes, they're charismatic, brilliant and sometimes downright inspiring – but at the end of the day, they're still just people. People with quirks, demands and the occasional temper tantrum over the wrong brand of mineral water.

This profession has gifted me with a wealth of experiences, an extraordinary lifestyle and a perspective on life that money simply can't buy. By writing this book, my goal was to pull back the velvet curtain, show you the reality behind the luxury and give you a front-row seat to the madness, the adrenaline and the moments that make it all worth it. If you've laughed, learnt something new, or simply enjoyed the ride, then my mission is complete. I hope this book leaves you entertained, inspired and perhaps a touch more curious about the world behind the scenes.

Postscript

I wish to emphasise that numerous inappropriate and unfiltered accounts in this book occurred during a period when I was an atheist, traversing an unfulfilled path, seeking meaning in all the wrong places. In retrospect, it is evident that I was lost. But I'm grateful to say that I have since found God, and my faith is now unshakeable.

I also wish to express my deepest gratitude to my exceptionally understanding and unwavering supportive wife. Without her strength and love during the latter years of my career, I truthfully would have existed in the past. Thank you for opening my eyes, providing me the grace to have evolved past my wildest dreams.

To the men reading this: I hope you discover your purpose. If not, confide in Jesus as your role model, He shall guide you.